ANIMISTS TO ANABAPTISTS

Establishing a Mennonite Mission
in Gambia and Guinea Bissau
2000 – 2013

Beryl Forrester

Partnership
Publications

Partnership Publications
www.h2hp.com

Cover art by Liz Hess

Animists to Anabaptists
The story of the Mennonite mission in
Gambia and Guinea Bissau 2000 - 2013
by Beryl Forrester

© 2015 by Beryl Forrester

Published by
Partnership Publications
A Division of House Publications
11 Toll Gate Road, Lititz, PA, USA
Tele: 717.627.1996

www.h2hp.com

ISBN-10: 0996292403
ISBN-13: 978-0-9962924-0-5

Unless otherwise noted, scripture quotations in this publication are taken from the *The Holy Bible, English Standard Version® (ESV®), copyright © 2001 by Crossway, a publishing ministry of Good News Publishers. Used by permission. All rights reserved.*

Printed in the United States of America

Contents

Foreword 5

1. The Lad's Lunch 9

2. Back to Africa 28

3. Extending into Guinea-Bissau 55

4. Life in Animistic West Africa 78

5. The Spiritual Itinerary 108

6. The Gospel is Cross Cultural 127

7. Forming the Community of Christ
   in the West African Animistic Context 148

8. Confronting the Lies of Animistic West Africa 182

9. In Retrospect

Epilogue: The Journey Continues 217

Appendix 222

Beryl Forrester has impressive gifts as a missionary of the gospel. His most important ability, in my estimation, is his open mind that allows him to wiggle into the culture of others. His open heart yearns to see people enjoy full salvation in Jesus within their cultures. It is amazing how Beryl's love for God and for people knows no boundaries. That love compels him to open his mind and heart to the challenges that face believers in all cultures. What he has learned in the many years as a missionary is astounding.

As you read this book you will be impressed, as was I, at the insights that God has given Beryl. He is a pioneer in the classical sense. He goes beyond where others have gone to plant gospel seeds in cultures not his own. The world needs more like him!

—Don Jacobs

Foreword

In my travels as a missionary, mission leader and coach, I have visited hundreds of missionaries and ministries around the globe. Airport terminals and the request to fasten my seat belt and put my tray in the upright position have become an ordinary part of life. But the trip you are about to take as you read about the life and ministry of Beryl Forrester in animistic West Africa will be no ordinary trip!

Rejected by three mission organizations and starting his long-term mission work forty years after his calling, Beryl has a story that reads like a modern patriarch "prepared for such a time as this" by his life experiences. Beryl helps us to see that each part of our lives prepares us for what God has in His long-term plans for us.

Beryl goes beyond biography to identify mission principles and practices and then illustrates them through real life stories. I hear many today talk about holistic ministry and justice for the marginalized poor. You will be introduced to the poorest of the poor in West Africa—the marginalized Balanta tribe—and how Jesus is transforming lives. You will see how the poor are not a "target of ministry" but rather a people to live among, accept and love with the transforming love of Jesus. You will discover some good missiology here.

But it may not be comfortable reading. Covers are pulled back on what masquerades as Christian ministry. Beryl writes about parallels between African animistic religion and the "self-gratifying Christianity" that is marketed today in Africa and beyond. Describing his own life journey, Beryl remarks on the shortfalls of "the American life" and how living in Africa has changed his perspectives.

I have engaged the common mission practices of establishing vision, developing goals, plans and action steps. Perhaps you have, too. Beryl's story will rock your world! He reveals how "vision was actually born out of mission, not mission from vision." All he had was a call: "Go to West Africa." He obeyed and stepped out in mission. Vision was revealed as he went.

Beryl is a pioneer and describes his ministry as pioneering work. Yet I love his humble, practical sharing and his willingness to say that incarnational work involves suffering, a word that many do not like to hear and most certainly do not like to apply. Because Beryl talks openly about the struggles of suffering, I want everyone engaged in pioneer work to read his book.

Do spirits exist? Is spiritual warfare real? Are people really held in bondage by spiritual darkness? Do missionaries change culture? Beryl answers these questions by describing the difference that scriptural truth has made in the lives of those for whom spirits and spiritual darkness are not "just a seminar" but real life!

You will see Jesus in this book. You will see him transforming lives. You will see how his kingdom is growing in The Gambia and Guinea-Bissau. I have walked with Beryl in the places he mentions and met some of the people he describes. I traveled those "taxis" with him. I have seen how he loves the people of West Africa and how he is loved in return. I have seen Beryl's love for Jesus and commitment to him. I have seen the growing faith of the believers.

When those talking of retirement make plans to "ease up a bit," I always think of Beryl. He started mission work in Africa at age sixty. His retirement home is an African-style house in Senegal, West Africa—one room with a bed, a sink, a table, two chairs. It's simple; it's Beryl.

At 74 he has slowed a little, but not much. He is still loving, accepting, and embracing West Africans and still sharing the transformational message of Jesus Christ. When Beryl's days on earth are done, I hope I am still around to join in celebrating his life, along with all those who have come from animism to transformational Anabaptist faith in The Gambia, Guinea-Bissau, and Senegal.

—Steve Shank, Pioneering Coach
Eastern Mennonite Missions
Salunga-Landisville, Pennsylvania

Chapter 1

The Lad's Lunch

It is fascinating to look back over the past seventy plus years and visualize my life as a 500-piece puzzle with each piece having a special place to fit in to make the picture complete. The story of my journey, starting in 1940 in Lowville, New York, has been choreographed by the Grand Composer, preparing me for my mission in West Africa. As the Psalmist says, "Your eyes saw my unformed substance; in your book were written, every one of them, the days that were formed for me, when as yet there was none of them" (Psalm 139:16).

Before delving far into this autobiographical chapter where I describe more of the puzzle pieces, it is disclaimer time. Nothing written on these pages should be construed as personal boasting or exaltation. My development and preparation for ministry in Africa is much like looking at the pathetic, laughable lunch basket of the five loaves and two fish the lad brought to Jesus as his contribution to a picnic of thousands of mouths to feed (John 6).

The disciple Andrew offers Jesus the feeble prospect on the miniscule resources available to feed the crowd, "There is a boy who has five barley loaves and two fish." He follows the proposal with an equally obviously rhetorical question with its implied answer, "But what are they for so many?" Jesus doesn't even bother to speak to the proposal: he simply orders the preparations to be made for the massive picnic. The tiny lunch basket turned into an unlimited supply.

That Bible story is an image of my life—just a lad who offers his life to the Lord. The lunch appears useless relative to the multitude of people needing to be fed, but Jesus multiplies

The author at age two with his parents, Charles and Kathryn (Jantzi) Forrester, and older siblings, Anna Mae Weaver and Dale.

the most meager offering if we are willing to make our lives available to Him. I really don't have much to offer but, "Lord, here it is." For that reason, the chapter's subheadings are titled fish or loaf to symbolize what I had to offer to the Lord. I do not propose any distinction between the fish and loaves.

If there is boasting, it is boasting in the Lord's power, not mine. I am just grateful I was naïve enough to offer the Lord my meager lunch.

In my adolescence, as I was in the process of taking ownership of the faith passed down to me from my heritage, my daily prayer went something like this: "Lord, my life is before me and I do not know now what all you have for me, but my life is in your hands; take it and use it as you see best for your honor and glory. Amen."

God has been faithful to the offering I made. My life can be viewed as a fortuitous coalescence of divine enablement with regard to my time, place and family of birth, education, job experience, friendships, economic growth, spiritual heritage, and many more facets of life. All of these things coming together, notwithstanding the blunders I have made along the way, enabled me to fulfill the design and will of God for my life, specifically to be a missionary in West Africa.

Fish 1: My Spiritual Heritage

I was born into a conservative Amish Mennonite community in Croghan near the northern part of New York. My maternal ancestors were among the initial settlers of that community when it was established in the 1830s by immigrants from the Alsace-Lorraine region of northeastern France. Although their roots were in the Emmental region of Switzerland, several generations of them lived in France before coming to America. As Anabaptists, they had been forced out of Switzerland by both Catholics and Protestants.

Although more than a century had passed since my ancestors' arrival in the New World, that independent, refugee, can-do, pioneering mentality was still palpable during my childhood years in the 1940s and 1950s. We raised most of our food, conserving it for the long winter, and our moms made much of our clothing. Most of the families in the community operated dairies, and my mom's generation still spoke the Low German dialect. A tight ethnicity was evident in our clothing styles and by our limited social contacts with the outside world. Socially and religiously, we were highly sectarian.

My dad, from across the border in Ontario, Canada, was from a Protestant family. Because he was the gregarious, extroverted type, he actually managed to jump over the sectarian wall and become a Mennonite, a relatively rare event in the 1930s. His momentum was probably assisted by the fact that he was in pursuit of my future mother, Kathryn Jantzi.

In search of better economic opportunity, he left Ontario as a teenager and migrated to northern New York State where he found work as a farmhand for a Mennonite farmer. Many of his buddies were Mennonite, and through that connection he met my mother. Her dad strongly disapproved and was ashamed of her courtship with a non-Mennonite, an outsider.

My dear mother, a staunchly pious Mennonite, did something I can scarcely imagine her doing, given how I remember her during my childhood years. On September 12, 1934, she actually kicked over the traces, hustled off with him, and was secretly married at the Methodist parsonage in Martinsburg, New York. For that she was summarily excommunicated from the Mennonite church.

Two years later, however, and with the arrival of my older brother, all came to a happy conclusion on a Sunday morning in August 1936 when my dad was among the baptismal candidates at the Dadville Mennonite Church. In the same ceremony, my mom was reinstated as a member in good standing with the congregation. Six years later I came along, but I was a teenager before I began picking up bits and pieces of my parents' story.

Prior to the 1960s the sectarian, conservative Mennonite community of northern New York stayed fairly intact. We had a deeply rooted Mennonite ethnic identity. It wasn't until many years later that I began to realize that particular identity probably wouldn't have been owned by our earliest 16th century Anabaptist forbearers and most certainly wouldn't have been owned by Jesus and his disciples. It was too ethnically based and, in effect, had more to do with shutting people out of God's kingdom rather than welcoming them in (Matthew 23:13). We were far more concerned about maintaining ethnic fences than focusing on obedience to our center, Jesus Christ.

It still puzzles me how our church leaders during the 1920-1960 era would have thought we could possibly be faithful in our responsibilities to the Great Commission, which they took very seriously, and at the same time maintain an 18th century Germanic ethnicity. It was a heroic, but costly, effort at serving two masters.

During the same forty-year period, we had yet another identity monkey on our backs. In the early years of the 20th century, a wide theological chasm developed between the conservative and liberal Protestants. Mennonites needed to choose which side they were on. At the time, our Anabaptist theological moorings were not well articulated and we had little to refer back to; we chose to be counted among the conservative Protestants.

Part of the conservative Protestant baggage was revivalism, which Mennonites embraced at the time. I was a good example of how that theology didn't compute with our Anabaptist understandings. In revivalism one had to get converted from unbelief to belief in God. The same template applied to everyone, whether an unwashed skid row wino or a kid in a Christian family: unbeliever becomes believer. This formula is problematic in that I was never an unbeliever. There was never a time in my childhood and youth when I did not faithfully believe all the essential doctrines of the

Christian faith. There was never a time when I didn't believe that God was Lord of my life, and always I wanted to be a disciple of Jesus. That is not to say I never sinned. I know very well that I did and I needed the power of Christ to be set free from ways of thinking and acting that are not Christ-like. I was in my middle years before I was able to unscramble that doctrinal rat's nest.

In reality, had our theology been better understood, we would have seen that we have little more in common with the conservative Calvinistic Protestants than we do with the liberals or even the Roman Catholics. In any case, identifying with the conservative Protestants brought us additional complications as we searched for our identity. It wasn't until after the 1950s that our own theologians and scholars began to put together a corpus of scholarly works that helped us to recapture many of the values of the radical reformers, our spiritual forbearers.

By the time I was ready to take up my Africa mission in the year 2000, I had schooled myself in Anabaptist Christology, ecclesiology, and missiology to the point where I was reasonably well- equipped to preach a holistic gospel and plant authentically Anabaptist-oriented Christian communities. In the years I have been in Africa, I have been studying in detail the volumes of the Believer's Church Bible Commentary as they became available. I have been helped, as well, by the writings of several non-Mennonite neo-Anabaptists, which started appearing late 20th century and early in this century.

As I ponder those centuries of Mennonite reclusive ethnicity, I wonder if God used them to preserve a people who would become leaders in a missiology that is so right for our post-Christian world. However all that is to be analyzed, I am most grateful to the Lord for my Mennonite heritage and how it equipped me for my work in West Africa. I could introduce you to a significant number of Africans who would share that same gratitude.

In addition to my spiritual formation, which I know will continue until the day I die, the Lord has been constructing numerous other building blocks throughout most of my life that were preparing me for the work in West Africa.

Fish 2: Compassion for the Poor, the Marginalized, and the Disadvantaged

Throughout my years in elementary school, I had a friend named Ronald. Every day he came to school in rumpled, oversized wool trousers held up by suspenders, the waistband in the region of his diaphragm. He wore a brown plaid shirt and had a speech impediment that made him difficult to understand. Moreover, he smelled bad and was always a loner. All these negative aspects drew me to him. I wanted to be his friend and get to know him. I never found out much about his family except that they were very poor and suffered from much illness. But he and I had a good friendship.

In my school there were many students like Ronald, children from broken, impoverished homes, living on the edge and without friends. The economy of our area of northern New York depended primarily on farming and forestry, with few industries or job opportunities. Although we didn't talk much about it, I suspect that poverty rates in our community were fairly high compared to other areas of the state that had well-developed business and industry.

My guess is that at least 20 percent of my schoolmates lived in poverty or were in some way marginalized and disadvantaged. In my heart, even before I reached my teen years, I was drawn to these people. Not that there was much I could do for them. I just sensed that they were suffering from some sort of brokenness. I saw mostly sadness and little hope or joy in their eyes.

Extending hospitality and care for the disadvantaged was very much part of the home I was born into. During my childhood, there were few times my mother was not caring for homeless children through the county welfare office. In her busy schedule, she even found time to be about the neighborhood tending to disabled elderly friends. My dad's hired farmhands were guys who drifted from farm to farm, unable to hold more responsible jobs. In my growing up years I had plenty of exposure to disadvantaged people, and somehow there was something right in reaching out to them.

During the 1960s, the U.S. government and social service agencies, including the church, sensitized us much to the presence of the poor and disadvantaged. While many well-to-do folks scoffed at this awareness and tended to blame the victims, I was happy to see a growing sense of social responsibility towards the marginalized. And while it is true that some programs to aid the poor were failures and in some cases even abetted poverty, still, there were countless cases of people being helped to a better life and well-being even by the much maligned "War on Poverty," which is the unofficial name for legislation first introduced by United States President Lyndon B. Johnson.

During this same period, several Bible scholars and theologians began making us aware that much of the ministry of Jesus was to bring good news to the poor, the downtrodden, and the marginalized. If you want to get close to the heart of Jesus, get close to the poor. We began to wake up to the social, economic, and political message of a holistic gospel. Getting people's souls saved, preparing them to go to heaven when they die (the message being preached in most evangelical churches), clearly was not the gospel preached by Christ and his apostles. Biblical salvation offers transformation and shalom to all aspects of human need and brokenness. Healing, wholeness and justice belong to the redemption we have in Christ, even today.

In the late 1950s when I turned 18 and finished high school, Uncle Sam had a plan for me. He offered a free education on how to rid the world of U.S. enemies by killing them and how to feel right about ending other people's lives for the supposed greater good of protecting the United States.

I respectfully declined his offer, but to his credit I will commend him for providing a reasonable alternative to us who believe we are here, like Jesus, to give life rather than take it.

When young men in North America were faced with the draft (compulsory military service) Mennonite leaders worked out a program that enabled conscientious objectors to military service to be inducted into an alternative humanitarian service program. During the 1940-1973 era, the alternative service program satisfied both the U.S. government and peace-loving Mennonites.

I served my obligatory two years in a program sponsored by MCC (Mennonite Central Committee), a relief, service and peace building agency of the Mennonite church. MCC assigned me to be part of an international peace building team in Morocco, North Africa.

This international setting was an enriching, life-changing way to spend my years between eighteen and twenty. I had opportunities to work with missionaries and several NGO's (Nongovernmental organizations) in medical work, refugee care and agriculture development in desperately poor, rural African settings. It was precisely the work I needed to be doing during those developmental years of my life. I learned to appreciate Africans, to be comfortable in a cross-cultural setting and I began to see much better how my life could make a significant contribution to what God is doing in our world.

During my preparatory years before returning to Africa, I embraced the message of salvation and began to understand why God had filled my heart with compassion for the downtrodden. Compassion is far more than humanistic pity; empathy belongs to the heart of Jesus' mission and is why he came to be among us. From day one, on my arrival in Africa in January 2000, I was intent on preaching the holistic gospel that transforms all aspects of human need and brings healing, wholeness and justice in Christ.

Barley Loaf 1: Education, Training, Job Experience, and Travel

The forty-year period of my life between my return from North Africa in 1961 and my return to West Africa in 2000 encompassed a wide variety of mid-life experiences and training, all of which proved to be most helpful in preparation for my third career as a pioneer missionary. Indeed, I cannot think of any of my activities during those years that did not in some way resource me for the work yet to come.

In 1961, during the last three months of my two-year term with Mennonite Central Committee (MCC) in Morocco, the Lord made clear to me that one day he would bring me back to Africa as a missionary. The Lord also made me to understand I needed a good deal more preparation and education than my high school diploma. Thus, when I arrived back in the U.S. in April 1961, I wasted no time enrolling at Eastern Mennonite University for the summer term that began two months later.

Before going to French-speaking Morocco I had two years of high school French, which enabled me to be reasonably conversant in French within the first six months there. By the end of two years, I was understanding and speaking French with ease.

In my college career, I wanted to continue French studies. Since EMU was offering only Spanish and German at that time, I had to go to James Madison University for French classes. Our French professor was a German lady who knew her French, but it came out with a heavy Germanic accent. With my advantage of having lived two years in a francophone country, every time she asked the class the meaning of a word or how to say something correctly, my hand was in the air. Since I always had the correct answer, the other students were a little intimidated. She finally said, "Jacques [we had to have French names], if no one else knows the answer then we will call on you; that way it won't be necessary for you to raise your hand." Even with that I still had to provide plenty of answers or correct the one that was given.

I give this illustration as an example of the multitude of ways, starting from day one (September 12, 1940), the Lord formed and prepared me for my task as a pioneer missionary. For example, there is no way I could have been a functional pioneer missionary in West Africa without fluency in French. Amazingly, every French word that I had learned during my youth stayed in my memory, even though I didn't use French regularly until my return to Africa forty years later.

Following undergraduate studies, I went on to the University of Denver and got a graduate degree in librarianship. During my youth, I had been an avid reader. As a child, if I was being looked for by someone in our household, the word was, "Well, you will probably find him somewhere with his nose in a book." My childhood home had some books, but not nearly enough to satisfy my need for reading material. Our church library and the public school library helped fill in some of the gaps.

Since I was reading before starting kindergarten, after two weeks there I was bumped up to first grade. Each year in primary school we were given a reading achievement test. By the time I was in grade six, my reading and comprehension level was grade 12. In my graduate record exam at the conclusion of my studies at the University of Denver, I was in the 90th percentile in language arts. In math, by contrast, my score was embarrasing. Theorems and axioms made absolutely no sense, but at least I could read and write. It was one of the librarians at EMU who looked me straight in the face and said, "Beryl, you should consider becoming a librarian." She was right; it was the perfect career for me.

I served as director in two rural public library systems, one in Vermont, the other in western Colorado. Both of those jobs helped me to develop my skills in administration, networking, and leadership, and I had exposure to collaborating with all sorts of people beyond the confines of the Mennonite world.

In the 1970s North Americans were caught up into a strong "back to the land" movement that grew out of the social upheavals of the 1960s. Although I didn't become a hippie, getting back to agriculture and deriving sustenance from the well-tended earth spoke to my agrarian Mennonite soul. As a librarian, I was set to become the first in my family lineage not to be connected to the land. I didn't want to be the one to interrupt that tradition.

So, in the wilds of western Colorado, on the west slope of the Rockies, I became the owner of a farm and at the same time continued my library position. Home was in the Colorado River valley, in an idyllic *Little House on the Prairie* setting within view of several fourteen-thousand-foot peaks of the Rockies. I had married in 1963, and my wife and I found the farm was the perfect place to raise two daughters. A few milk goats, bee colonies, and chickens shared our small farm. Home was a snug sandstone house built by Italian immigrants two generations earlier and heated by coal from a mine less than a mile away.

By 1978, however, I was ready to move on to other things and get back into a somewhat more functional Mennonite community than we were experiencing in Colorado. We headed northwest to the Willamette Valley of Oregon, and I bought an operating fruit orchard, including an antiquated simple farmhouse where we lived until my return to Africa in 1999.

When I bought that farm in 1978, I left my library career and became a full-time fruit grower. Orcharding suited me much better than the dairy farming of my childhood. I found trees, fruit, and the permanence of the orchard much more manageable than contending with wily, simple-minded livestock. As an orchardist, I learned much about agronomy and fruit tree culture, preparing me for work with African subsistence farmers with their depleted soils and survivalist agriculture.

Owning farmland in the later decades of the twentieth century was a good financial investment even if I didn't make much from the farm production. My land investment appreciation was a key factor in my ability to become a financially self-supported missionary.

During those twenty years as a fruit grower, I held various positions in the church, including pastoral elder in the local congregation. I also served on the district conference mission board and edited the district conference quarterly paper. I was active in the Willamette Valley MCC relief sale, providing apples and cider for that event. All these activities—farming and church responsibilities—provided me with priceless experience in ministry, business, and community development that directly contributed to my skills and maturity in preparation for my return to Africa.

Fruit growing tends to have a cycle of highs and lows of work requirements for maintaining the orchard. The busiest time was between bloom in March and harvest concluding in July. During that period, I normally worked seventy hours per week. For the rest of the year, there were many orchard maintenance requirements, but my schedule was fairly flexible, with times of minimal activity. While one doesn't become wealthy as an orchardist, the rhythms of orcharding afforded two major benefits of which I took full advantage: solitude for reflection and study and blocks of free time allowing me to travel internationally.

Some social scientists would have us believe there is a gender linkage between men's proclivity to jumping the fences and exploring the abroad and beyond. While the woman is at home nurturing and tending the household, her man is out foraging and wandering. Or maybe wanderlust is a holdover from Cain's punishment that he would "be a wanderer on the earth." Whatever its origin, I had it bad, especially since my return from North Africa in 1961. From that point onward my self-perception has been first and foremost international. Being an American or a U.S. citizen is of no consequence or value to me emotionally or psychologically. My first loyalty and identity is citizenship in the kingdom of God, and I am at home wherever I can do the most for the coming of God's Kingdom.

During the 1980s and 1990s, I made seven bicycle tours through numerous European countries and at least that many short-term mission trips to the Caribbean and Central America with either Mennonite Disaster Service (MDS), Youth with a Mission (YWAM), or independently. These all were just temporarily whetting my appetite for the day when I would be free to be abroad full-time. My international travel made me comfortable and confident that physically, emotionally, and spiritually, I would do well overseas.

During my forty years away from Africa, I daily wondered why it was taking the Lord so long to open the way for my return. The librarian and farmer carried on frequent conversations with the Lord about how I could be doing so much more for his kingdom if I were back in Africa rather than developing library resources and tending an orchard in the U.S. He reassured me that my work during those years was also for his kingdom, that this was all in preparation for that next phase, and that the return to Africa would happen when the time was right.

Barley Loaf 2: Work Ethic

All my ancestors came to northern New York State as penniless, landless peasants. I am not aware that any of them or their posterity became wealthy by North American standards. Most became owner/operators of their family dairy farms by the second generation. None have gone beyond a lower to middle class net worth. I am grateful to belong to a heritage like that. All of them were very hard working souls, undaunted by the long pull ahead, yet none of them became Horatio Alger heroes.

When I acquired my fruit farm in Oregon, I had open land ready to be planted to trees. I planted a 15-acre site to hazelnuts. The tree stock came from a nursery a few miles from my farm. The day I planted the orchard I picked up the nursery stock in lots of 1,000 trees each time. The nurseryman was aghast when I came back late in the day for the last 1,000. He exclaimed, "Someone must have taught you how to work!" I said, "Yeah, my dad was responsible for that."

When I returned to Africa, I took along that hard work ethic. I continued working ten- to twelve-hour days although I was at the beginning of my seventh decade. That ethic served well in getting the mission up and going with a fairly extensive program during the first five years even though it was a one-man mission team. Much depended on my skill of organizing and involving locals in the work plus my own 6 a.m. to 10 p.m. schedule.

By the time I was pushing seventy years, however, I was noticeably slowing down. That was good because by then we had a missionary team of anywhere from five to ten expatriates plus local workers. I needed to back off and allow people with youthful vision and energy to take over. I welcomed the diminishing workload.

Barley Loaf 3: Thy Kingdom Come

The number one passion of the Christ and, by association, that of his disciples, is to see the kingdom of God coming and his will being done on this earth as it is already being done in heaven. God's holiness and shalom have absolute sway in heaven; that righteousness and glory are in the process of enveloping and transforming our world as it eternally comes under God's rule. Disciples of Jesus have no other vocation than joining together with God in this great work of salvation. That is the worship/service that I bring to God as a disciple of Jesus. As a missionary, this is the transformation I wish to be happening in my own life and to facilitate in the lives of others.

Salvation that authentically transforms people is possible only through the power of the Holy Spirit, but he uses our hands, feet, and mouths to move the process along. As a missionary I have witnessed this transformation happening in the lives of people. Two aspects of the process intrigue me: Where does the journey begin? And how does one know it's for real? Perhaps these are among the mysteries we will never quite figure out in this life. Still, I wish to know as much as I can about it.

We find many clues about the kingdom's arrival among the teachings of Jesus; these fascinate me. In John 7, Jesus is confronting unbelief and opposition among the Jewish religious leaders. In verse 17 he says, "If anyone's will is to do God's will, he will know whether the teaching is from God . . ." Here Jesus is giving primacy to one's will. A resolve of the heart to be doing God's will and being part of his kingdom precedes, or at least accompanies, one's coming to faith in Christ. Without that resolve, the seed that is sown is quickly eaten by the birds or is overtaken by the fast growing thistles.

I have seen this phenomenon among seekers in West Africa. Those who are authentically seeking new life in Christ as an alternative to the oppression of animism will find it. To them, peace and the light of Christ are beautiful and welcomed alternatives to the darkness, sadness, fear, and pain of the animistic worldview. They have resolved in their hearts that the righteousness of God is what they authentically desire.

Sadly, many African seekers come from below, desiring Christianity for self-centered reasons, hoping that a Christian identity will be the path to power, riches, and honor. Only when seekers have resolved to submit their will to God, live in obedience to Christ, and join the community of faith for kingdom purposes, are they able to grow in knowledge and faith and realize victory over sin.

We had a couple who associated with the mission for several years and in some ways were helpful in generating interest for evangelism in many villages. I noticed, however, that no matter how much teaching they received, it never produced spiritual growth and fruit. Eventually their ulterior motives became obvious as their sham disintegrated into ashes, and they openly began opposing the gospel.

I have offered my life—my lunch basket, such as it is—to Jesus for the sake of God's kingdom. That is that model I desire to see replicated in the lives of those our mission reaches with the Gospel.

Chapter 2

Back to Africa

Oregon to The Gambia
November 1999 – March 2005

The first signs that the doors were opening for my long-anticipated ministry in Africa came during the final weeks of the 20th century. On a typically overcast November morning in Oregon's Willamette Valley, I had just made my ritual trip down to the mailbox and was returning to the house when a white extended-cab Ford 250 diesel pickup turned into the driveway and slowly growled its way to where I was standing near the garage.

The driver leaned his head out the window, greeted me and asked, "Is this farm for sale?"

I said, "Yes, it is, but it would be best if you could come back in two weeks so I can show you around and we will talk about it more then." After a bit more conversation, I suspected I had a serious buyer, prepared to make a deal.

And so it was that by the end of November 1999, my assets were liquid, and I was free to return to Africa and begin the life and ministry I had been dreaming about and for which the Lord had been preparing me during the previous forty years.

What I wasn't seeing in those days of closing out one epoch of my life and moving into the next was the scale of what was ahead and the enormity of the opportunity God was placing before me. In my small mindedness, I envisioned myself returning to Africa to work with some farmers at improving crop production and along the way to share my faith with those who might be open to learning more about Jesus.

Simply put, the vision was "Go back to Africa, do some agricultural work and share the story and the love of Jesus." Period.

In my thoughts and imagination there was not even the hint of Mennonite Church West Africa, an EMM partnership, a missionary team, clinics, preschools, agriculture projects, business enterprises, mission compounds, village fellowships, and whatever else has transpired. It is a case of the vision growing out of the mission rather than the other way around.

I also figured that a seven- to ten-year stint in Africa would probably assuage the longing of my heart for Africa and that I would return to North America. It was a satisfactory but very limited vision. In hindsight, I realize what I had in mind only betokened God's plan for me as a servant in the extension of his kingdom.

How to get back to Africa and inaugurate the work the Lord had for me was also a subject of some evolvement. Having started out in Africa under MCC, a Mennonite service agency, I assumed that my return to Africa, whenever it took place, would also be under a Mennonite mission. At least that's the way I thought it should be. But as the time before any future service in Africa lengthened into decades, I began to see that my next service was unlikely to happen through a Mennonite mission agency. Time and the vicissitudes of life reduced my likelihood of meeting the expectations of a Mennonite mission.

Eventually it became clear I needed an alternate plan to get back to Africa, one that depended primarily on something the Lord and I would figure out together. Nevertheless, I did investigate serving through three different Mennonite agencies, and as anticipated, I was politely turned down. But that helped me to know that the venture of getting back to Africa was something that needed to be put together by the Lord of the harvest, myself, and a few close supporters of my vision, with a little help from a parachurch organization.

An aside: I wonder if the day will ever come when human resource offices of mission agencies might have a special portfolio labeled "The Called but Unqualified." It is where, for example, they would file applications from people like the Apostle Paul.

Even before the Oregon farm sale happened, I had applied to Youth with a Mission (YWAM) concerning a short-term volunteer opportunity to serve on the Mercy Ship Anastasis in Banjul, Gambia. In their first response to me, the door with YWAM was not open; all their volunteer slots for the Anastasis ministry in Banjul were taken. However, at about the same time the orchard sale was happening, I received a letter from YWAM saying there was a cancellation and that, indeed, they did have a place for me on the ship docked in Banjul. To take that position I needed to be in Gambia by January 25, 2000. I had just enough time to close the sale, vacate the property, and get my travel plans in order.

So, how does an independent pioneer missionary with a vision of going to Africa proceed to bring the vision to reality?

Step One: Take Stock of your Resources.

God, in nudging Moses to be a leader of the Exodus, got Moses' creative juices flowing by posing the fairly simple question, "What is it you have in your hand?" What did I have in my hand? My in-hand inventory included these:

- A clear call from the Lord of the harvest to report back to Africa for a ministry he had there for me, together with a burning, nothing-will-stop-me determination to be obedient to that call.

- My stateside family obligations were minimal: my daughters had families of their own and my wife and I had gone our separate ways. In response the Lord called me to celibacy, and that enabled me to devote myself wholeheartedly in service to him.

- The encouragement and prayers of my immediate family, my fellowship group at Salem Mennonite, and a few other long-haired, John the Baptist-type visionary friends.

- Sufficient personal financial resources to get myself to the field and provide maintenance while there and a perch for when I arrived (on the Anastasis).

Step Two: Get a plane ticket and go.

With those formalities out of the way I arrived on board the Anastasis docked in the Banjul, Gambia port on January 25, 2000.

I loved the Anastasis. It was an ancient tub that had started life as a transatlantic passenger vessel in the 1930s. In World War II, she was co-opted as a troop carrier, and by 1970 she was on her way to the scrap iron furnace. Luckily for her, she experienced rescue and a rebirth as the Anastasis through the vision of YWAM's Mercy Ships ministry.

The Anastasis was built in the era when much of a ship's interior was still made of wood and other combustible materials that don't do well when exposed to either fire or water. With numerous incidents of both on the Anastasis, the carpentry/repair crew was kept busy, dealing mostly with water damage.

During each of my three short terms on the Anastasis, I was assigned to the carpentry shop crew. Our shop was in the very bottom of the ship, five decks below main deck and far below the waterline. Gratefully, we didn't spend much time there, but each day I made numerous trips into the cavernous depths leaping down companionways in three bounds and racing through narrow passageways with my repair materials and tools in hand. Although the year 2000 was my year to turn 60, I was as nimble-footed as any of the young men on the crew.

While my service on the Anastasis was totally enjoyable and I loved my shipmates, I wasn't wired to become a card-carrying YWAMer. YWAM has its roots in the Jesus freak/charismatic revival movement in the 1970s; I am a died-in-the wool, cradle Mennonite. Although we share lots of Christian camaraderie and community and do mission together, we are still not quite at the same street address. YWAM even has a tamed down, geriatric DTS (discipleship training school) for people like me. But that was still more cookie cutter than I was prepared for. So I simply served with YWAM as "volunteer associate crew."

My time on the Anastasis afforded me service opportunities in addition to routine repair jobs like resetting hinges on doors and digging up water-ruined carpeting. These after-hours ministries proved beneficial in providing connections on land as I left the ship and began the first stages of the mission in Gambia.

One opportunity was to volunteer to be a companion to persons coming to the ship for surgery. After my work day in carpentry, I was able to spend time meeting my patient, visiting with him, explaining his procedure, answering his questions, hearing his story, encouraging him in his faith and praying with him. The nursing staff gave me the francophone patients because I am reasonably fluent in that language. Through some of these patients, I was able to make connection with Gambians as I inaugurated my work in Gambia.

For example, there was Yaya, who came for facial repair surgery. He was a penniless man in his mid-twenties from the Casamance region of southern Senegal. Because of an untreated infected tooth, he lost part of his upper jaw and ended up with an opening into his mouth through his cheek. With this disfigurement he lost his pride and any sense of self-worth. In his family and village, he was regarded as demon possessed and something less than human.

Yaya wanted desperately to come to the Anastasis for plastic surgery but didn't have the fare to go from the town in Gambia where he was staying to where the Anastasis was docked in Banjul. Fortunately, he found a kindhearted Muslim man who had a job at a gas station in the neighborhood and provided him with the fare. Yaya was accepted for surgery, and when his turn came for the operation, I was assigned to be his companion during his hospitalization and the follow-up visits. Yaya knew nothing about a loving Father God who understood all about him and wanted to bless him with healing and a new life. He enjoyed hearing stories of Jesus, the One who came to help us fully understand God and bring healing to our lives. I spent a lot of time with Yaya, even visiting him at his family home. The family had connections in the Gambian village of Jalambantang that provided me a venue where I later began a ministry to a preschool. I also helped some of the farmers there with crop development.

I also met his friend at the gas station, Sulayman, who provided the fare for him to come to the ship. That meeting started me on a friendship with Sulayman who was instrumental in helping me find my way to his village, Pirang, Gambia, after I left the ship. Sulayman helped me secure land in Pirang where we established a Mennonite mission center. He also introduced me to the Balanta people in Pirang. Ministry to that people group eventually took us to Guinea-Bissau. A significant amount of the mission's ministry is traceable to this friendship formed during my three months on the Anastasis.

The ship also hired about fifty Gambia residents, called day workers, as staff for the ship kitchen, housekeeping, ship maintenance and translation for patient care. The day workers are recruited as part of the Mercy Ships' advance preparation for a ministry. Mercy Ships administrators are diligent about involving local churches anywhere the ship docks for medical ministry. Local pastors recommend day workers, people from their congregations who will benefit from several months of training and interaction with the Mercy Ship crew.

The Banjul day workers were most eager to form friendships with expatriates on board, even though their goal may have had ulterior motives such as securing financial favors or finding a track for emigration. I welcomed their friendships but was always mindful of their propensity for ulterior motives. Most of these people were refugees or clandestine residents in Gambia from other West African nations. Most were Christians but seriously in need of friendship, discipling, and mentoring. They all had fascinating life stories.

These men helped me immensely in my education about living and working in Africa. I learned much about how to work successfully with African culture and personalities and also about West African churches and their version of Christianity. They were my missionary orientation boot camp, and for my first years in West Africa they were my primary mission focus and Christian community. At this juncture in each of our lives, I needed them and they needed me. Most of them have left Gambia, but I maintained friendships with them long after leaving Gambia. Sometimes when I am in Banjul, I occasionally run into one of my original buddies.

Sam was one of the Gambian day workers I grew very close to. He was from a nominal Catholic family who all eventually converted to Islam. Sam, however, got involved with a graceless, legalistic, authoritarian Nigerian evangelical mission that only added to his confusion and sadness. A brilliant, competent man, he was still very lost. I did what I could to help him know God who loved him, forgave him and could bless him with the peace and wholeness for which he so much yearned.

In our conversation one day, he looked at me and said, "Dad [as they all addressed me], I have something important I need to tell you. You have sacrificed much to come here to share Jesus with us and help us with our hardships. And I know God is going to do a great ministry through you that will eventually extend to a large area of West Africa."

At the time I was too dumbfounded to make any kind of a sensible response, but in retrospect I realize that though weak in faith and probably unclear in his understanding of God, he nevertheless spoke a prophetic word to me that did indeed portend of things to come. And while I didn't share his confusion, I also was weak in my faith, and I, too, needed to grow in my understanding of the power of God as a missionary God.

My term with Anastasis ended April 30, 2000. My time on board had provided an awesome launching pad for an independent pioneer missionary who had neither a mission board nor any missiological oversight for these first tottery steps toward establishing a mission.

The most significant learning for this launch period was a principle that would guide me through the coming fourteen years as a pioneer missionary: Look for the people who are looking for God. The two groups I ministered to on the Anastasis—the day workers and the patients coming for surgery—were desperately searching for spiritual moorings, spiritual identity, and a secure faith locus. They needed what I had to offer: the Messiah who comes to make all things new and is inviting us to join him in realizing God's kingdom and will on earth as it is in heaven.

Before leaving the Anastasis phase, I have a few points of interest yet to toss into the story.

One has to do with taking note on the various ways God provides for his people to do mission and ministry. For myself, I need to serve in a clearly incarnational milieu and model. I need to be with (as in live with) the people to whom I am ministering. I may not be quite as incarnational as a "Bruchko", but still I need to be there sharing life with my people group.

I found the Anastasis ambience a really awkward way to do mission. The ship not only resembles a cocoon, it literally is one. Here you have this tiny, armor-plated, impregnable, sanitized, floating capsule of Western culture, connected to, but not quite part of, the vastly different world of impoverishment and wretchedness. This oasis of bliss, plenty and comfort, peopled by happy, fun-loving missionaries was within yards of a teeming slum of human misery, suffering, and depravity.

From my do-it/live-it theological tradition, it wasn't easy to sit through extended services of exuberant praise, prayer, and worship in the cocoon, knowing that just a skip and a jump away, outside the thin skin, I had brothers, sisters, and lots of little kids who were enduring an existence that wasn't fit for a dog.

This is not to pass judgment on anyone, just to take note that there are varieties of styles in mission and ministry. I feel a whole lot more comfortable getting as close as I can to doing it the incarnational Jesus way.

The other item is the story of a close brush with disaster on board the Anastasis. Just after midnight on a still February night, everything on the ship was quiet, including the groggy watchmen. The chief engineer suddenly woke from a deep sleep to hear an urgent voice in his brain saying over and over, "Go to the engine room, go to the engine room, go to the engine room. . . ." He leaped from his bed, pulled on his clothing, and raced to the engine room, which was several decks high. To his horror, as he looked up into the scaffolding of the engine room ceiling, he saw the place was ablaze—in close proximity to where all sorts of explosive petroleum products were stored!

He immediately pushed the abandon-ship button, and the ominous sounding siren literally resurrected all 400 of us from our slumbers. We scrambled along our well-rehearsed evacuation routes towards the gangway and out onto the dock. Even the hospital patients were evacuated. The only ones remaining on board were the intrepid firefighters.

The ship was equipped with a trash-burning furnace with a three-foot diameter flue that passed through all the decks, including a storage deck where unsupervised workers had stacked cardboard and plywood boxes against the flue. The trash burner was seldom used, but when it was, the flue could get red hot because of the draft and trash inside it. That's how the fire got started just above the engine room. The firefighters soon had the flames doused and the area cooled. But everyone knew we had come within moments of a major catastrophe in the life of the Anastasis.

As we huddled in small groups on the dock outside the Anastasis, we prayed, sang, and chatted for more than an hour until it was safe for us to re-board and get back into our bunks. In my heart the promises of Psalm 121 became a lot more real through this near tragedy: "Behold, he who keeps Israel will neither slumber nor sleep. The Lord is your keeper . . . The Lord will keep you from all evil; he will keep your life."

Serekunda, Gambia
May 2000 – March 2001

During the first ten months after leaving the Anastasis, I settled into a two-room apartment in the London Corner district of Serekunda, Gambia's largest city. I was still functioning under the somewhat limited vision I came with: Find a church or training center where I could assist in Christian formation and work with subsistence farmers.

I remained deeply involved with my friends, the former day workers of the ship. I met with several of them weekly, sometimes daily, helping them sort through some of their perversities and helping them to know Jesus. They continued teaching me the ins and outs of being a pioneer missionary in West Africa.

An important learning for me during this period is the validity of the ministry of presence. It happens when a person, mature in faith, spends time with another believer, or even an unbeliever, struggling with issues of self-worth, finances, moral compromise, bereavement, and numerous other enigmas of life. It's a presence that conveys, "I am here with you, I believe in you and value you even though we are different. I know life is not easy for you, and I also know there is hope." Being present with people in this way opens the possibility for them to draw life from my spiritual resources. It's a way of sharing the presence and power of the Holy Spirit as he flows through me to others who hunger and thirst after God.

As I have walked alongside many discouraged, marginalized, wounded people in West Africa, I have often thought: If I don't accomplish one more thing in my ministry in West Africa, it was worth it being here if only as a presence of Christ, for these, my friends.

My day-worker friends took me to their churches, and I joined in their services and met their pastors and leaders, most of whom were Nigerian, Ghanaian, or Sierra Leonean. Most of these church communities were AIC (African Initiated Churches).

In all these churches it was rare to find Gambians as pastors or in leadership positions. One exception was the Family Celebration Center whose lead pastor was a well-known figure in the Gambian Christian community, even in Gambian politics. But he had been trained in Nigeria and was still closely tied into his Nigerian support network. One of my day-worker buddies who was an usher took me along to a service, a special weekend revival with some high-profile preacher from their Nigerian base.

A high point in the service (I hesitate to call it worship) was to have the big cheese from Nigeria present the Gambian pastor with a set of keys to a black Mercedes, not a new one, but still a handsome, elegant set of wheels. It would look great parked in the driveway of his villa in the upscale Fajara part of town. At least one needs to give the man credit for living the gospel he preaches.

A crowd of 250 was there for the Saturday evening service, probably half of them young men under forty. The teaching was about how the Lord was just waiting to bless them, make them successful leaders, and provide for their financial abundance. The preacher somehow managed to find an Old Testament character as a model, I don't recall just which one, on whom God had poured out these blessings. Nothing was said about Jesus. He didn't get a mention until later when high-powered prayers demanding God to do this, that and whatever else were finalized with a loud "In the mighty name of Jesus!"

Long before this, I was casting about looking for my closest exit. Leaving these services early wasn't easy, especially for a white visitor whom the usher seated in a special row of chairs up front. However, I had been to enough of these events that I was wise to all this and didn't allow the usher to seat me up there. Finally, at one juncture in the service when the chaos level was sufficiently high, I managed to flee, relatively unnoticed, through a nearby exit.

On another occasion one of my friends took me to his church, part of the Winner's Chapel denomination. First he took me to see the facility and meet the leaders. It was only a ten-minute walk from my London Corner flat. These people were in the process of building a sprawling mega church complex and were using it even though it was less than half complete.

Both this church and the one in the previous story had a member taxation system, requiring communicants to reveal their income and pay a ten percent tithe on that amount. All this was recorded by the church treasurer's office. Every Sunday the congregation was hammered about paying the tithe. Scriptures were quoted to back up tithing as an obligation and as a threat if one failed to pay up. Nonpayment could line one up for God's judgment in the form of sickness and misfortune. Besides the obligatory tithes, there were the voluntary offerings if one really wanted to bring down God's blessings. All this has shades of African animism, with which I would later become very familiar.

Winner's Chapel was holding a revival and healing campaign featuring another big name from the circuit of miracle-working evangelist teams from Nigeria. Vivid handbills were pasted up around town, advertising the weekend opportunity for healing, deliverance, and blessing at the Winner's Chapel. At Taja's insistence, I accompanied him to the Sunday afternoon special healing service.

Hundreds of people were seated around all four sides of the vast gymnasium, and on the floor in front of us was the crowd of people who had been recruited to come for healing. They were a noisy, unruly bunch, some of them mentally deranged and not seeming to have much understanding of what was going on. There was every type of sickness and handicap imaginable. Then I realized someone had gone to great efforts to round up all the sick and handicapped that one encounters on a visit to the Serekunda market. Here was this motley crew of the lowest rungs of Gambian society all brought together for a miracle service in front of us spectators, all as a witness to the miracle-working power of the worthy evangelist.

First was a short message on how God was about to perform great signs and wonders. Following that, the sick were required to repeat a prayer which apparently made them sufficiently Christian to qualify for a faith miracle. Then the ministry crew went from one sick person to the next, gesticulating and praying over them, demanding God to heal this person and pronouncing them healed in the name of Jesus.

Again, for me, this was all such a farce and a travesty of the Good News of God's kingdom, that I soon found my way out of the auditorium and headed back to London Corner.

In the months following my departure from the ship, I had occasions to visit a variety of churches. I was looking for an opening where I might fit into a ministry that was truly seeking to be obedient to the prayer of Christ that his followers would help to usher in God's will and kingdom on earth as it is in heaven. However, I was finding myself on one deadend bunny trail after the other.

The Call to Establish an Anabaptist Mission

One day in early 2001, about a year following my Anastasis term, I was walking along the beach in Bakau, adjacent to Serekunda, thinking about how my ministry was developing and feeling a certain level of frustration. I had a desire for something more structured and goal-oriented and was becoming more and more disillusioned with what I was seeing among the evangelical/charismatic AICs. In spite of all their efforts, I wasn't seeing God's kingdom coming and his will being done as it was in heaven. I wasn't seeing the suffering servant/new creation ministry modeled by Jesus. This just wasn't happening anyplace where I was looking. Instead I was seeing a charade of men of flesh bent on building their own fortunes and names by abusing the Name that is above every name.

It was there on that deserted beach that I heard a distinct but inaudible voice saying, "The Africans deserve something far better than what they have in the array of churches and missions you are seeing here. They need to see and experience the option of a radical community of Christ, an Anabaptist-oriented community of believers serious about being Jesus' disciples." From that moment on, I knew God wanted me to grow my vision and begin planting a series of Anabaptist-Mennonite fellowships in the villages where I had already begun agriculture extension work.

A Rural Ministry

Through my friendship with Sulayman and Yaya, I began to work with women's community gardens already established in the Kombos region of Gambia about twenty miles southeast of Serekunda, along the Gambia river. One area of contact was five miles south of Brikama around the village of Dimbaya on the Senegal border; the other was five miles east of Brikama in the village of Pirang.

I was traveling out to these areas at least weekly from my residence in Serekunda. In several villages I did what could be called agricultural extension work with women in their community gardens and with individual farmers who asked for my assistance as word spread about my availability. I brought seeds for new vegetable varieties and did citrus grafting with stock from California. It didn't take long until I had all the contacts I was able to deal with while maintaining my mentoring relationships with the former day worker guys in Serekunda. I was busy all my waking hours seven days a week tending to the ministry opportunities the Lord brought my way.

I used public transport to reach Brikama, a fifteen-mile trip. I kept a bicycle at the Methodist mission in Brikama to visit villages around Brikama. A country boy by nature, I found my contacts in the villages more appealing than what was happening in the city of Serekunda. I sensed my ministry moving in the direction of the rural opportunities.

One day as I was leaving Dimbaya on my bike, I was hailed by a man who came running up asking if I would be able to look at his okra planting. Since the sun was already getting close to the horizon and I needed to hurry back to Brikama, I promised to visit him on my next trip to Dimbaya. He introduced himself as Andre. That raised questions in my mind. People in this predominantly Muslim culture were not given a Christian name like Andre. When I asked him if he was a Christian, his answer was yes.

On my next visit to Dimbaya, I found Andre and his farm a few hundred feet across the border into Senegal. In addition to getting a tour of his farm, I had more discussion with him about his faith. He told me that in their village were Senegal people who were Christian but not involved with a church. I asked him if they might be interested in Bible study and worship and, indeed, they were. So the next Sunday in March 2001, I met with them under a tree just outside the village of Dimbaya on the Senegal side.

It was a group of about twenty-five persons, mostly nominal Christians and certainly more animistic than Christian. But they wanted to learn more about Jesus and be taught the Bible. That group of believers, still active in Dimbaya, became the first Mennonite fellowship in this region of West Africa encompassing Gambia, the Casamance area of southern Senegal and the Cacheu region of north Guinea-Bissau. It is the Mennonite fellowships of this region that were eventually affiliated with EMM in 2005.

One of the first things they asked me to do, in addition to gathering them together for worship, was also to serve them communion, which I gladly did, even though I knew full well their faith at this time was minimal and probably mixed with other beliefs. At least they were reaching out towards Jesus in the best way they knew at the time.

While this was happening in Dimbaya, positive developments were shaping up in Pirang about five miles to the east. Pirang is the village of Sulayman, my Muslim friend who was instrumental in helping me get the mission started in Pirang. There, in addition to working with farmers, I was also involved with a group of parents eager to have their children in pre-school.

Sulayman helped me secure 2.5 acres at the edge of Pirang, adjacent to the village rice fields. It was a site the villagers regarded as the haunt of spirit beings. No one would pass through that property after dark. But for the Mennonites—no problem. It was a great location to start our mission, especially once we staked our claim and told those creatures they needed to be gone. The village elders gave us a 99-year lease on the site with only one stipulation: You must not build a church. Again, no problem. We didn't need to build one; we were it. Anywhere Christians are working together, the church is there, with or without an edifice.

Working with the women in their community garden endeared the mission to them and built a solidarity that doesn't go away. Also, when I listened to the parents tell about their desire for preschool education for their children, another solid relationship bridge was built.

I told the parents that the mission would furnish the materials if they would furnish the labor for the building. An additional condition was that since the mission was Christian, it would be necessary to teach about Jesus in the school. We weren't aiming to convert their children from Muslim to Christianity, but we wanted to hold Jesus as an example of how God wants us to live. The parents had no problem with that stipulation.

The school opened January 2003 with about 100 students and three Christian teachers. As children completed their years at the mission preschool and went on to the public elementary schools, they were at the top of their classes because of the good preparation they received in the preschool.

In the classroom of the Mennonite pre-school in Catel.

The men of the village also aided us in the construction of the mission center on the property leased to the mission, the former abode of the spirit critters. In January 2003 I was able to take up residence at the mission center in Pirang.

In late 2002, I was in conversation with Jeremiah Sillah, a Christian student at the Gambia College agriculture training center in Brikama. After completing his course in the spring 2003 semester, Jeremiah joined me at the Pirang mission center to work with the agricultural program. He eventually became a co-director of the Mennonite mission in Gambia, the job he currently holds.

Another important development during these early years was getting registered as a non-governmental organization (NGO), giving the mission legal status with the Gambia government. The registration process took almost two years, but in 2004 we finally had NGO status as Mennonite Educational and Horticultural Development Associates (MEHDA).

Although we attempted to register the Mennonite church, that process has not been successful. The official government agency that registers churches is controlled by the three original denominations left over from the colonial era (Catholic, Methodist, and Anglican). For their own reasons, they are unwilling to share the playing field with other Christian groups even though new AIC church groups have proliferated in Gambia.

In Gambia our church is known as Gambia Mennonite Church and is part of Mennonite Church West Africa, an umbrella for the Mennonite work in southern Senegal, Gambia, and Guinea-Bissau.

Early on in my time in Gambia, a Mennonite brother in the U.S. challenged me on the way I assumed the use of the Mennonite label, especially since I was not officially appointed by a Mennonite agency. However, no one has a lock on that name. Few people in this part of West Africa had ever heard of the term "Mennonite," but they were favorably impressed with the one Mennonite they knew. Faced with the need for a label for the mission that was developing, I knew "Mennonite" was by far the best choice for this West Africa scene.

As I have gotten around a bit in West Africa, I made friends among pastors and missionaries who value the Anabaptist witness once they get acquainted with our theology and missiology. Among these contacts are Sam and Elizabeth Bello, a Nigerian missionary couple who came to Gambia a year after I arrived. He was sent to Gambia to work in a mission that actually didn't pan out for him. When we got acquainted and I shared with him my theological perspectives and a book by John Driver, his reaction was, "Why, this is exactly how my wife and I understand the Bible. We had no idea there was a denomination that had this theology!" Sam and I partnered in rural missions for several years until he needed to return to Nigeria.

I have experienced a bit of that reaction at various places I have touched down in West Africa. There is a certain knowing on the part of some thoughtful, sincere believers that the Christian church in West Africa has wandered far from the vision and Spirit of our Founder. These people see a sign of hope with the presence of the Mennonite witness in this part of the world.

Changes on the Home Front: Pennsylvania Becomes my Base

With the establishment of the Pirang mission center in 2002 and the beginning of our first two village fellowships in Pirang and Dimbaya, the Mennonite mission was well on its way to taking on a life and identity of its own.

Throughout this early period, I made at least yearly visits back to the U.S. Home base for me then was Oregon, where I had lived for twenty years and had many connections with the Mennonite community of Oregon.

However, it was my brother-in-law and sister, Robert and Anna Mae Weaver, in Lancaster, Pennsylvania, who had most enthusiastically taken up the stateside banner for the fledgling Mennonite mission field opening in Gambia. During my visit to Pennsylvania in 2002, I became a member of their congregation, New Holland Mennonite Church, and thereby also a part of Lancaster Mennonite Conference. I was subsequently credentialed by Lancaster Conference for the ministry in West Africa. With this transition, my locus of support and interest in the U.S. moved from the west coast to the east, centered in Eastern Mennonite Missions (EMM) territory, a milieu far friendlier to overseas mission than the one I had experienced in Oregon.

In the early years of 2002-2004, as the mission was growing, I was beginning to see it would need a supportive constituency. I could see that the work was becoming something far larger than my original vision of being simply a personal ministry on my part. Visiting in the U.S. and telling my story of the developing West Africa mission drew a warm reception in Pennsylvania; naturally, I gravitated towards more promising potential of support in eastern Pennsylvania. Because I grew up in New York State, had my Lancaster connections as a youth, and attended Eastern Mennonite University, I was well aware of the East Coast Mennonite ropes.

A significant stateside task during the first five years was making people aware of the Mennonite mission being raised up in West Africa. Mennonite churches I had been affiliated with had for years been supporting missions in East Africa. West Africa was new territory. Among my Mennonite connections, I had a major public relations gap to fill.

One of the ways of working at that gap was to invite people to make short-term mission trips to visit us in Gambia. Having short-term visitors and youth teams from the U.S. has been a feature of the mission since fall 2003. In 2004-2005 I was able to host two youth teams at the Gambia mission from Rosedale Mennonite Missions. The many short-term visitors and youth teams we have had over the years have had the cumulative effect of making the West Africa mission field a reasonably well known entity in the Mennonite heartland.

YESers assisting at a Bible study at Catel Mennonite.

Coming Under the EMM Umbrella

Ron and Judy Zook, pastoral couple at New Holland Mennonite Church, developed a keen interest in the mission, and with their enthusiasm and encouragement, the congregation became the primary support group for the work. It was through Ron's endorsement and connections that the mission eventually became part of EMM in January 2005.

When I was visiting in the U.S. in 2003, I made a stop at EMM in Salunga, Pennsylvania, (near Lancaster), but Clair Good, the man I needed to see was not in the office that day. Clair was the Africa Area Representative for EMM.

The following year on my visit to the U.S., Ron and I had some serious conversation about the mission's need to be connected with a mission agency, specifically EMM. Ron had even accompanied a visitor group to Gambia, getting firsthand knowledge of our efforts there. A few weeks later, Ron and I landed a meeting with Clair in June 2004 that got the wheels turning in the direction of the Gambia mission becoming part of the EMM global family and for me, personally, to become an EMM appointed missionary.

In late 2004, Clair visited our mission in Gambia. He was impressed with our interaction with the Gambians and he liked our simple, low-key incarnational mission model and that I personally had invested in the mission. He returned to the EMM head office in Pennsylvania with a positive report and a recommendation to the Board. He told the EMM executives that while the West Africa work had its risks, it appeared to be a suitable candidate as an EMM mission venture. It helped that I was a member of an EMM/Lancaster Conference congregation and that the congregation was already interested and committed to the mission. It was also significant that I had my support system already in place. The mission met other EMM criteria: it was working with an unreached people group, was developed around a holistic gospel approach, and we were using traditional EMM methodologies. At their board meeting in December 2004, the board took official action to subsume the West Africa work into the EMM worldwide program, with me as mission director. All of that became a reality in January 2005.

Conclusions

In the initial five-year period of developing the mission, these were some of my learnings:

1. It is reasonable for an individual, independent of a mission board, to take the lead in establishing his ministry and mission. Church agencies such as mission boards serve many useful functions for the church, but it is all right to think, plan, and act outside their box. In fact, it is normative to act outside the box particularly when the Lord is preparing a pioneer missionary and directing you to establish a ministry that is essential for the advancement of his kingdomn in an unreached area.

2. A limited vision is enough to start with, but don't be bound by the limits of your vision. Be fluid enough to give the Spirit ample room for change and bigger things. If you feel too small for the task, don't worry, God will provide the human and other resources needed for what he wants to accomplish.

3. Be sensitive to the profundity and shape of the lostness of those to whom you are ministering. The missioner's response to spiritual needs must be calibrated against the faith development stage of your people group. You come with a message and a theology but your theological baggage may need some reshaping to make it understandable by your people group.

4. When going about your ministry, whether it is in the establishment phase or even later, there are three essential door openers: Go with lots of smiles and be openly friendly. Get in touch with the other's needs—spiritual and physical. And go in a spirit of humility and servanthood. Do these and you will

virtually never have a door slammed in your face, especially in West Africa.

5. Be aware that three aberrations of Christianity are seriously impeding and threatening the development of faithful, Christ-centered discipleship communities in West Africa:

- The appeal of the prosperity gospel preaching that plays so forcefully on the vulnerability of the poor and powerless.

- The relative difficulty of Africans to abandon traditional religious power in favor of the power of Messiah Jesus who has already put an end to Satan's dominion. The social pressure to maintain animistic customs is enormous. Most churches have given in to this heresy and allow their members to keep a foot in both worlds.

- A heretically inadequate Christology that perceives Jesus as merely a mechanistic stepping stone for individual souls to magically and effortlessly gain heaven.

Chapter 3

Extending into Guinea-Bissau

In July 2005, Antonio Peda, a Balanta man from Catel, Guinea-Bissau, was visiting his family in the village of Medina near the coast in Gambia. Behenia (the village name means 'the angry one") was helping his host family gather wood out of a wood pile to cook the evening meal. Unknown to the men, a spitting cobra had taken refuge among the branches on the ground. As Antonio pulled out a branch, the startled cobra reared up and spit its venom into Antonio's eyes.

This is how the spitting cobra immobilizes its small animal prey so they can be consumed. Cobras don't consume people but they do spit in the eyes. Although the venom is not fatal, it is important to profusely flush the eyes immediately after the attack. This will shorten the period of pain and limited vision and prevent permanent damage to the retina.

The next day, when we were in Medina to hold a weekly service with the villagers, Antonio came for prayer and treatment. Soon the swelling of his eyes went away, and his vision returned to normal.

Most of the people we were ministering to in our Gambia village fellowships were Balanta refugees from Guinea-Bissau. When some of them began to experience the joy and peace that comes with being in Christ, they had a natural desire to share the good news with their families and friends in Guinea-Bissau, 70 miles to the south.

We had discussed with the Balanta church leaders in Gambia the possibility of starting a mission in Guinea-Bissau. There was unanimous affirmation by the church in Gambia for this move. From the beginning of the movement into Guinea-Bissau, the Gambia brotherhood understood the effort as an extension of the Gambia Mennonite Church and desired to have a contiguous relationship with whatever developed in Guinea-Bissau, homeland to most people involved with the Gambia church.

Suddenly, voila, the link we needed to Guinea-Bissau was sitting right there in front of us in the person of Behenia. I learned as much as I could about his village, Catel. He assured me there wasn't already a church there and warmly invited us to come to Catel where we would find a welcome and could easily get land for a mission center

I invited Behenia to our mission center in Pirang, Gambia, and began teaching him about Jesus. The Pedas are dedicated animist and I am doubtful that much of what I was saying was getting through. Still, he listened attentively and made appropriate responses. During those early years of the work in Catel, Behenia helped organize church services and in many ways was a good host. But he never did make a break with animism and become a disciple of Jesus. He is an example of one whom the Lord sends alongside and who graciously facilitates in the early stages of church planting. Although he is a friend of the church, he never actually gets on board.

In mid-September 2005, I sent my Balanta coworker on ahead to scout out the turf around Catel and make some initial contacts. I joined him in Catel during the last days of September.

Getting down to Guinea-Bissau from Gambia means traversing the Casamance region of southern Senegal, a trip of about eighty miles. In 2005, a low-level guerilla war of twenty-five years was just winding down. Sporadic outbursts of shelling, highway robberies, and random murders were still happening. Although we never directly encountered any danger or threats, the risk was clearly there. The route down through Diouloulou and Bignona and on to Ziguinchor was (and still is) heavily guarded by the Senegalese army. After Ziguinchor the route leaves Senegal at Mpak and enters Guinea-Bissau at Jegue.

In Catel, where we were guests of the Peda family, everyone in the village knew we had arrived to begin some kind of work. In the period from September 2005 through April 2006, my coworker and I spent two to three weeks each month in Catel. We discipled seekers and began establishing fellowships within cycling distance of Catel.

I stayed with the Peda family in their large house of mud brick walls and compacted dirt floors. Sometimes I had a room to myself; sometimes I had to share the bed with Behenia, depending on how many people were home at the time. The bedroom was only about eighty feet square, most of the space occupied by an ancient iron bedstead. The mattress, lying on the slats, originally was ten-inch light duty latex foam. But after years of use, the center area of the mattress had compressed to a mere two inches thick from the body/bodies gravitating to the center.

That meant, in order to avoid rolling down hill into the center of the bed, up against Behenia, I had to sleep with one arm hooked over the edge of the mattress, holding my body firmly in place on the hillside of concaved foam.

Although the Peda family was among the least industrious in Catel, their father/grandfather was one of the original Balanta settlers in Catel, probably in the 1950s or 1960s. Their longevity in the village made them a family of status even though they were very poor. The more ambitious Peda progeny moved off to Bissau, the capital city, and have salaried jobs. The ones remaining in Catel are clients of their urban kin. When I visited family members in Bissau, I listened to complaints of how the men of the family in Catel sat all day with their arms crossed, which, in fact, was true. But at least, they are preserving the family's village roots, an important factor in keeping the ancestral spirits placated.

When I arrived in Catel, a process began to unfold that happens every time a missionary or community development worker goes to inaugurate a village ministry. It happens regardless of the color of the missionary's skin but probably is more intense when one is white.

One doesn't just march into a village, set up camp and start preaching. Socially and culturally, he first needs an introductory meeting with the community leaders and anyone else from the village having an interest in this contact.

Because every community has hopes for outside contacts, the arrival of someone from the outside is a major event. It is automatically expected that someone coming from the outside will be bringing gifts and benefits to the village. I think there is no way to avoid going through the process (unless one stays in North America and pretends the rest of the world doesn't exist).

It doesn't matter how directly and forthrightly one says, "No, I cannot build you a new school or hospital, I am not going to be giving sewing machines to the women and I am not going to be providing the men with fishing nets." Simply coming to a village and talking about development automatically triggers hopes and expectations of things that one may do for them. It's all part of the interaction that happens with outsiders. In their view, bringing good things to them is part and parcel of what a missionary who comes to a village does.

How often was I told the story of a certain Italian man who came to the nearby village of Kincha and built a school, and so, "Forrester, when are you going to build us our school?"

These expectations are driven by four well-embedded, cast-in-concrete, worldview factors:

1. There is the hard historical evidence that people from far away, missions, and NGOs bring good things and development essentially as handouts. It impinges on everyone in the village to jump up and quickly get in line for the freebies. This may be a once-in-a-lifetime chance. Grab while the grabbing is good.

2. This culture, like most African cultures, is a patron-client society. An important life goal for everyone is to find his place in relation to persons with greater social status, more political power, and more wealth than they have—something like a sugar-daddy. If someone is open to this sort of relationship

with you, it is important for you to find ways of showing him honor—boot licking, as we would call it colloquially.

If he allows you to do that to him, he becomes a patron. Goodies now come straight from his hand. The more honor heaped on the patron, the more he is obligated. The more honor dished out to him, even if it is sheer flattery, earns favor credits.

When the missionary comes around, he is honored with a gracious welcome to the village. He is offered land. Everything is done to show him honor, knowing that shortly he will have earned his patron badge.

If he fails to deliver, then he is shamed, because this is also a shame-honor culture. Shaming is a major social/behavioral control tool. I've been through it all many times over: "Forrester is bad, bad, bad. He promised to build us a clinic and till now we see nothing." They were still saying that even after the clinic was built and in full operation. Already their families had repeatedly received medical services from the clinic they actually helped build.

3. A third sad but true worldview factor is that many Africans perceive themselves as second class; they can't solve their problems but only create more of them. Anything they do is of inferior quality and merit. I will leave it to the historians, the sociologist, and the ethnologists to fix blame for this low self-esteem; nevertheless, it is there. When the development practitioner, the missionary or NGO comes around, it is important for the recipients to grovel in their incapacities.

4. Finally, a survival mentality drives much of life and relation-
    ships in this part of the world. How am I going to make it
    through life? How will I have food for tomorrow? These are
    questions close to the surface for the individual, the clan, and
    the village. The survival mentality is a key factor in social
    interactions. Here there aren't the governmental or economic
    safety nets to protect against disaster or destitution. The only
    safety net is what can be put together through a social or
    familial network.

All the above were happening as we sat with a large crowd of
Catel villagers under the central cashew tree that late September
day in 2005, the beginnings of the Mennonite mission in Catel. I
was given time for a short message from the life of Jesus. I don't
recall the exact text, but it was something about how Jesus offers
us the opportunity for new life and relationship with God and each
other. It is God who brings transformation to our communities,
recreating us into the original design for his creation. Everyone
listened attentively.

After that, however, it was their turn to present me with their
laundry list of projects they expected me to bring to their village: a
skills training center, a community garden, a new school, a clinic,
an ambulance, fishing equipment for the men, a soccer field for
the youth, a church and a few more things.

The mere fact that I was present and listened to their wish list
was in itself a commitment to bring all these things to Catel during
the coming months. That's the way they understood our meeting.
That was their missionary job description imposed upon me.

This dream lives on in the hearts of many Africans even though their landscape is littered with the decaying remains of that failed development strategy: schools without teachers and educational materials, empty clinic facilities, crumbling cashew roasting ovens and the rusted hulks of farm tractors.

Our first years in Catel were a playing out of their development aspirations that could lead only to failure versus our philosophy that while the missionary could offer partnership in development, the primary engine for development is Africans taking responsibility for their own development and using the resources God has already put in their communities.

Although it took all of five years, numerous projects were getting underway in that period which would begin to work at some of the root problems. We executed the projects in ways that at least partly fulfilled the goals of local ownership and utilization of community assets in resolving the road blocks to transformation. All of these initiatives still needed lots of refinement and growth, but at least we had made a beginning in five ministry programs.

1. Early Childhood Education: Few children were learning to read and write even after four years in primary school. Lack of qualified teachers, small or non-existent teachers' salaries, little or no educational materials (books and classroom furnishings) and scarce classroom discipline, were all responsible.

    The mission didn't have the resources to adequately deal with any of these deficiencies, but there was another way to skin the cat: Put the children through three years of preschool, preparing them for the primary school experience. This orientation to educational discipline and their eagerness to learn facilitated the educational process and maximized the meager primary school resources.

The preschool, under the guidance of expatriate missionaries, is a notable success with eager scholars in pajama-like uniforms and parents pleased at the change they see in their children. The primary school teachers love teaching these kids who

A child at the Mennonite pre-school in Catel. Because they are better prepared, students who attend preschool are much more successful in primary school.

had been to the preschool and were now ready to learn. The school district was so encouraged by the results that they gave permission to have the preschool on the public elementary school campus. They also asked one of our pastors to teach Christian values in the other four elementary class levels.

2. Cashew Processing: Guinea-Bissau has only two agricultural crops produced in sufficient quantity to enter the world market: cashews and peanuts. Until now, cashews have been exported as a raw, unshelled nut, transported to India for processing. Not only is the raw product exported, but so is the potential for reaping the economic benefits of value-added processing. However, technology is now available to do processing of the kernels in-country, thereby creating another level of employment in addition to grove maintenance and harvest. Adding

value to a product in-country logically is going to help the GNP.

The Mennonite mission got into cashew processing in 2010, helping three men in Catel with the purchase of hand operated shelling machines and guiding them in the establishment of a cashew processing business. This venture has great potential for creating jobs at the village level. As the business evolves both in technology and management, everyone wins. Our project, joining with several other small processors, is able to produce enough volume to enter the global cashew market.

The challenge this program brings is putting together a work force that understands what it means to participate in a profit-making business operating on proven business practices and also embracing Christian values. Employment means one shows up for work five days a week at 8 a.m. and works until 5 p.m., one doesn't walk off with the company product or equipment, nor does he use his place in the company as a resource to maintain his client-patron network.

Many adult men in Guinea-Bissau understand their role as passing most of their waking hours socializing and drinking tea or wine with their age-mates in the shade of a cashew tree, attending "choaras" (ceremonies honoring the ancestral spirits), and producing progeny. A man who does those duties has met at least 90 percent of the expectations put upon males. In their worldview, spending most of the day, six days a week, working for wages is truly an alien concept.

3. Permanent Cropping: Guinea-Bissau has but one perennial, permanent tree crop under cultivation: cashews. Although,

Guinea-Bissau isn't strictly monocultural, it comes close to qualifying for that designation. Everywhere you look there are cashew groves, thousands upon thousands of acres are planted to cashews. And that is virtually the only crop, permanent or annual, aside from small plantings of peanuts. Consequently, the economy does reasonably well if the world cashew price and the weather are both favorable.

This limited crop variety has an even more negative result: The ground that should be producing a rich variety of food crops for a complete and wholesome diet for the local population is instead producing a crop that adds to food variety and nourishment of people far, far away. It's a kind of agricultural colonialism by people and market forces far from the control of those hurt by such a policy.

The Mennonite vision for mission has a strong justice component: God's kingdom values challenge injustice, even in relation to food production and distribution. It should not be surprising that on the mission farm we have a planting of three permanent tree crops that do very well in Guinea-Bissau: a grove of cultivated palm oil trees, a citrus orchard, and a soft wood forestry planting. All of these crops are perfectly suited to the climate, soil and water resources of the area. They are a living testimony to God's goodness and the richness of his creation. In addition they will be part of the future support of the mission as the church becomes sustainable from local resources.

4. Community Health and Access to Medical Care: During our first months in Guinea- Bissau, late 2005 to March 2006, we

were still only part-time in Catel. We always traveled there from Gambia with a good supply of medicines. People began showing up at my door with wounds to be dressed and infections needing antibiotics, while others were suffering with malaria, parasites, and skin fungi.

Dr. Jonathan Yoder consults with a patient at the Mennonite clinic in Catel, which is blessed with assistance from many short-term medical professionals from North America. The clinic is directed by Tening Mane, a nurse trained in Senegal and who is part of the leadership team at Catel Mennonite.

Armed with my volume of *Where There is No Doctor, The Merck Manual*, and a copy of the *Nurse's Drug Book* we did what we could to help those with medical needs. There were raised eyebrows at EMM when they learned about the extent of my medical practice, but the care given relieved much suffering and brought healing to hundreds of people who came seeking help. In so many cases the healing went beyond what one would normally expect from the level of care we were able to give. To me it was clear that the Lord was there, filling in the gaps of our limitations. Ministering in this way, in the name of Jesus, is what we are called to do.

Most of the people coming had no access to medical care. A vast amount of physical suffering was the result of the lack of medical access and treatment for fairly simple, routine illnesses.

General ignorance about healthful living and disease prevention accompanies an animistic worldview. That understanding provides no linkage between illness, physical injury, and well-being on one hand and causative infectious organisms, random accidents, and sanitation and health maintenance on the other. An animistic worldview says that when I am ill, have an injury or an ulcer that won't heal, it is because someone has placed a curse on me and there is demonic activity going on against me. I need to take action to intervene against the curse, find out who is doing it and put a greater evil on that individual.

Beginning in 2008, we were getting short-term medical professionals among our visitors from the U.S. and it was a great relief to turn medical treatment over to people who had far more training and expertise than I did. By 2009, we were having nearly full-time coverage from short- term medical professionals. We opened a small clinic office in a corner of the meetinghouse at the mission center and kept somewhat regular hours. The health ministry got a big boost through the short-term ministry of Annette Miller, RN, and her husband Jon, a pre-med student.

In February of 2010, I attended a four-day conference in Accra, Ghana, designed to introduce CHE (Christian Health Education) to potential networkers. My invitation to the meeting was thanks to Sam Bello, my Nigerian missionary friend in Gambia.

I was the first Mennonite that Sam ever met. He was quite taken by Mennonite hands-on, implicit theology and our vision of a holistic gospel. One of Sam's daughters was a secretary for the West Africa CHE office in Nigeria, and Sam made a strong pitch to the CHE director, Dayo Obaweya, that the conference needs to hear about the Mennonite way of doing mission.

I was asked to present a case study to the conference on the Mennonite mission philosophy and our ministry in Gambia and Guinea-Bissau. My presence at the conference put me in touch with numerous organizations, including Heartbeat for Africa and Medical Ambassadors International. Out of those associations, I connected with Ron Pust, a professor at the University of Arizona Medical School, Tucson, Arizona. Ron oversees the school's international medicine curriculum. Those connections resulted in Ron's coming with two groups of his international studies med students, one group in 2011 and the second in 2012.

The med student group in 2011 did village health surveys in five villages where we had ministry. The results of these village surveys provided us with the rationale for the medical program we were to develop. It confirmed our suspicion that most children between three and seven, while not malnourished, have stunted growth from lack of a balanced diet.

Ron, active at Tucson's Seventh St. Presbyterian, has a warm spot in his heart for Mennonites. He had a 1950s Lutheran upbringing in the boonies of eastern Montana in the town of Big Top. Big Top was also home to a Mennonite community. In the 1990s he connected with Dr. Glenn Brubaker at the Mennonite hospital in Shirati, Tanzania. Ron sent some of his students to Shirati for their international practicum. He was happy to bring his international medicine students to the Mennonite mission in Guinea-Bissau.

In 2011, the Catel clinic services were moved to the cashew processing building when the cashew project was temporarily stalled. Terianne Edwards, RN, gave a year of service as the medical provider and did much to raise the image of the clinic in the community. The cashew processing building was redecorated and organized into a functional clinic.

Another building block for the establishment of a self-sustaining clinic operated by Africans has been the nurse's training project for Tening Mane. Tening was among the first group of young men in Catel to show a commitment to following Jesus and to be discipled. He has a keen interest in ministering to the sick and is committed to following Western medical protocols in treatment of the sick. When Tening's training in Ziguinchor, Senegal, ended in October 2013, he assumed responsibilities as director for the clinic and other health programs of the mission. Into the future, the mission will likely be seeking the assistance of expatriate medical professionals to work alongside African health care givers.

The mission's medical ministry seeks to be much more than simply curative treatment. We have a larger vision for improving community well-being and preventing infectious diseases. To help us in the promotion of healthful living we have become part of the CHE (Community Health Education) network. The CHE approach helps communities take responsibility for their own development and transformation, first using the resources already available in the community. A partnership with outside organizations is still an option, but only after the community owns its problems and establishes a plan to address its needs with its own resources.

The mission became a cooperator with CHE in 2010. CHE training was offered in Catel in 2011. The training equipped church members to organize the CHE approach in villages where we have ministry.

The CHE organizer assists a village committee to name the three or four most significant problems that are impeding development in the village. The committee selects maybe a half dozen villagers who will serve as the local training and action group. These people will be trained in lessons which will help the villagers address their problems.

For example, if some of the problems are the lack of prenatal care and infant mortality, the trainer from the mission will give the village trainers already prepared lessons in prenatal and neonatal care. Once the village trainers have been equipped with the lessons, they will present the lessons to every household in the village.

The international CHE network has literally thousands of lessons on every imaginable topic. The lessons are all biblically based and they are presented in a participatory learning format, rather than strictly lecture.

By 2012, we were assisting three villages where we have ministry in using the CHE resources. The mission, Medical Ambassadors International, seconded Lia Viega, a Brazilian missionary, who helped us establish the CHE program.

5. The Establishing of a Christ-like Community of Faith

From my early days in Gambia in 2000, it became obvious to me that without spiritual transformation other arenas of development could not be sustainable. For me, authentic development means following the design of the Creator in relation to any sphere of human endeavor, be it economic, social, educational or agricultural. Life must be ordered according to the will and design of him who made our universe and all of life. We come to know God's will for life and its many relationships thru a covenanted inner spiritual relationship with the One who created this real world we live in. And that relationship needs to be joined with other Christ-followers in the context of the community of faith.

Thus, it is not surprising that within hours after our arrival in Catel, I was inviting people to a Bible study on the veranda of the Peda house. There I told them about Jesus who came to live among us to show us how God wants each of us to live in relation to himself, our Father. That restored relationship informs and transforms how we live with those around us and how we participate in the beautiful creation he has given us to care for.

I didn't cover all that in the first lesson, but that is the basic outline of how we perceive the good news of the Gospel of Jesus Christ. Some missionaries begin with Genesis chapter 1, explaining to their hearers how sinful they are because of their rebellion against God; an angry God is portrayed whose holiness has been offended by mankind. That is followed by God intervening, sending Jesus to die in our place and for us on the cross. While all that is true, it is not the Good News transformational itinerary used by Jesus.

We start with a God who loves us so much he gave his Best to bring us back to himself, sending his Son who lived just like any other man, except that Jesus lived his life in total faithfulness to God. He defeated the powers of evil, even death, and is ready to share that transforming victory with those who are willing to become disciples of Jesus.

We focus on Jesus who comes to establish the kingdom of God through disciples who are transformed into the lifestyle of Jesus and who desire to live out God's will on earth as it is in heaven. In Catel, we are inviting people to become the new people of God, to become a community of Christ-like persons through the power of the Holy Spirit.

To shepherd animistic people from the darkness and slavery to Satan into becoming faithful disciples of Jesus is a slow process. But once they begin to experience the joy of living life the way God created us to live it, many are eager to be liberated from the satanic slavery that holds sway over much of West Africa.

A worship service at Catel Mennonite Church

It took several years of discipling the first seekers before any of them were ready to renounce the powers of Satan in their lives and publicly become followers in the way of Jesus. But that was a solid beginning for the formation of Christian community in Catel.

These five ministry programs had their beginnings during the first five years of the Mission as it was being established in Catel, Guinea-Bissau. There have been several bumps in the road along the way to evangelizing in the way Mennonites have understood evangelism from our Anabaptist beginnings nearly five centuries ago.

We experienced opposition and obstacles on at least two fronts. One, the concept that many in the village hold about development is that once you have your white man missionary in the village, you own him, and he is obligated to develop the village. He will magically and effortlessly bring the good life of the West and make everyone as wealthy as he is.

We went through that scene many times to the point where the village Youth Association demanded the keys to the mission and told us to pack up and leave the village immediately. Fortunately, the Lord provided some cooler heads in the local government who didn't allow that to happen.

Second, we had our share of persons feigning Christianity with the covert agenda of enriching themselves on what they thought was our largess and ignorance. The problem with that pretense is the reality of Christ's warning: "By their fruits you will know them" (Matthew 7:16). The make-believe can be maintained for a period of time, but then the rotten fruit inevitably begins to show up.

Both of these trials, while not easy, helped to strengthen the church against the wiles of the devil in what must be one of the world's most difficult mission settings. We observed the wisdom of the Apostle Paul as he reminded the Corinthian believers there is a positive side to the unfaithfulness of some "in order that those who are genuine among you may be recognized" (1Corinthians 11:19).

An unanticipated benefit of having community development projects is that these projects assist in the discipling of the new believers and the long process of developing local church leadership. Those who are being groomed to be church leaders, persons who build up the body of Christ, are involved with the day-to-day operations of the projects: the cashew processing, pre-school, clinic, farm and other mission-initiated enterprises. As these leaders mature in their spiritual walk, they concurrently become more responsible, progressive and innovative leaders for the community development projects; as they become more faithful disciples of Jesus, their business and managerial acumen is nurtured and refined at the same time.

We give all glory to God as we were honored to participate in the coming of his kingdom in this corner of his creation.

The Mission's Physical Facilities

Carrying out these ministries required at least a minimum physical plant for the Mission. After some weeks with the Pedas, we were able to secure a house along the paved highway through Catel. The house was owned by the chief of Bandera as a location to purchase and store cashews. He invited us to use the house rent free temporarily.

During the early weeks of our involvement in Catel, the Peda family talked about giving the mission a two-acre tract of land. However, that never happened because the head of the family who made the offer died in early 2006, about three months after our arrival in Catel. His children did not share his generosity, and the offer was withdrawn. Instead, they sold the mission a plot of land 75x25 meters. On that site we built a mud-brick structure 12x12 meters as the mission center. The mud bricks for the building were made by the village Youth Association. The construction was started in April 2006 and was under roof by the time the rains arrived in mid-June that year.

The building was the typical Guinea-Bissau style with a veranda on all four sides and a four-slope zinc roof. Two-thirds of the floor space served as our meeting place, and one-third became a three-room mission staff living quarters.

With the leftover mud bricks from that project, we built a 20- by 20-feet structure immediately behind the meetinghouse. This served in various capacities over the years as a storage shed, clinic, living quarters, and cashew processing facility.

The construction was carried out by local masons and with the help of volunteer crews from the U.S. The cost of these first two buildings was less than $5,000.

We were able to begin using the facility by mid 2006 even though construction was not complete. Sitting down on rough planks stretched across mud bricks, we held worship services and Bible study sessions even before the floor was poured. That, somehow, seemed better than sitting under a cashew tree or on someone's veranda. Before the end of 2006, we had a floor, the walls were plastered and whitewashed and we had backless benches to sit on. We always preached from an ordinary table rather than a pulpit.

When the Peda family's offer to furnish a tract of land was not realized, the Nhanca family offered a nearby three-acre plot of land at the edge of the village. This land was much better although it was a bit farther off the highway. On that land we built our fourth and fifth structures.

First was the mission house to provide housing for missionaries. This 10x20-meter building included a common room and five bedrooms. It was built in 2007 for about $11,000 with the help of local masons and volunteer builders from the U.S. It is built with locally fired bricks, which are more resistant to termite infestation.

One hundred feet from the mission house we put up a similar size building, also made of fired bricks. This fourth building has served as a cashew processing facility and a clinic.

Expatriate Missionary Staff

During the early years in Bissau, we maintained a significant presence of expatriates in Catel. The visibility of expatriates was an important factor in the establishment of the mission. It portrayed a significant level of commitment and involvement in the region. The locals were accustomed to seeing missionaries come to their villages for a couple of hours, and then disappear, never to be seen again. We were not that kind of mission.

When we went to the village to share the Gospel, the inevitable question was, "Are you going to leave us too?" Our well-established mission base in Catel and the mission team signaled that we were serious and would be there for the long term. We were careful to nurture a strong incarnational model among the expatriate staff that communicated, "Yes, we are from far away and we have a white man's culture, but still, we are present here in the village with you. We don't require anything special, we are willing to live simply beside you, and we want to be involved in your lives."

We were socially accepting and interactive with everyone in the village who was open, friendly, and welcomed our presence. In this part of Africa, openness, hospitality, and welcoming the friendly visitor are a cultural expectation. The motivation for the friendly welcome may be coming from an agenda we found difficult to understand, but still the welcome mat was out and we responded positively.

We saw three types of expatriates sharing in the work at Catel. A few of us were long-termers, committed for several years with the mission. There have been only two long-termers during this period: myself (here for the duration) and Andrew Stutzman who was here 2009–2014.

Then there were the EMM YES teams and GO! volunteers who spent three to twelve months with us, and then finally, the visitors who came for a couple of weeks. Significant bonding between nearly all the expats and villagers was abundantly evident. The locals talk positively about specific persons who were close to them from among the forty or so expatriates who have been on the Catel team.

The expats played an important role as models and signs of hope in a culture where most people are looking for someone from outside to show respect, interest, and care. In Guinea-Bissau, a country very near the bottom of the HDI (human development index), an incarnational, empathetic presence is a welcomed, powerful witness to God's love and grace.

Chapter 4

Life in Animistic West Africa

The story of Sabado highlights significant aspects of life in an animistic society. When she and her husband parted ways, Sabado continued to live with her three children (ages 8, 11, and 13 years) in their house across the street from the Mennonite church in Catel. The husband moved on to another town and another woman.

As often happens in a neighborhood, her children quarreled with the children next door. In this case, the family next door was that of the village chief.

One day when the children were sharply disagreeing and exchanging insults, the mothers became involved. The Muslim chief heard his wife and the woman next door verbally attacking each other. He was unable to go immediately to the aid of his family because he could not interrupt the ritual prayers he was engaged in at the moment. But once he was free, he rushed next door and the conflict quickly escalated into physical blows.

What really happened, who hit whom and how hard, will probably never be known. The result, however, was that Sabado came out of the battle paralyzed, with a serious wound to her lower back. Most of the villagers think the chief used demonic powers in his assault on her.

Sabado languished in agony for weeks, gradually losing strength and the will to live. We ministered to her with prayer and medicines. Her sister faithfully changed the dressing for an abscess on her lower back that grew to a diameter of ten inches and refused to heal. At one point, we transported her to the regional medical center, a reasonably well-equipped and staffed facility. We were told there was no way they could help her.

The family moved her to a bush "hospital," a center operated by a herbalist/sorcerer. There she lay in a small hut and took traditional treatments, but to no avail and soon she passed away.

Her death was considered a murder. Although the chief was taken into custody, he was back home within a few days, his release arranged by a relative in the justice system. He needed only to report in at the police station every Monday in a village about twelve miles away. Then he was free to come back to the village and resume his duties as chief. After a few months, his records were totally cleared.

However, at the time of this writing, for Sabado's family, the matter is not over yet. They have a solemn responsibility before the ancestral spirits to determine who is culpable in Sabado's death. To ascertain who used witchcraft to cause her death, there will be a séance, presided over by a witch doctor, at the sacred tree in the village. The parties gathered will include Sabado's family, her former husband, and the chief.

Libations of wine will be poured out for the ancestors and the other demonic powers. Many prayers will be said to the idols posted under the sacred tree. The officiating sorcerer will kill a rooster, pouring out its blood to appease the ancestors.

Then each of the three participants will select one of three small organs from the rooster—the sex organs, the bile duct, and a short section of intestine. The sorcerer will remove the organs selected and carefully examine each one. If the organ contains a blemish or bloody spot, the person selecting that organ will be deemed the guilty party who used a spell to cause Sabado's death. Within a few hours, the guilty person will be expected to either drop dead or go insane. And untimely deaths will continue in the family of the guilty one.

Animism

This story illustrates how life in animistic West Africa is lived in ways that are contrary to the harmony of God's created order. Interactions between persons and between people and the environment violate God's design for his creation and include intense marginalization of women, broken family relationships, economic poverty, a disregard for basic human rights, and degradation of the environment.

Consider a few more dimensions of life in this animistic setting:

- Life is primarily combative; peace and tranquility are the exception. Little children barely able to walk, will without provocation wobble up to one of their age mates and hit them—pow!

- There is an overriding need to dominate the other. Confrontations always end up in high decibel name calling and curse shouting that can go on for hours and frequently come to physical blows. However, given a few hours or a day or two and the combatants are joking and laughing and having a great time together. Of course, the scars and mistrust remain.

• Personal and family honor are of first importance. Rendering first aid and medical care to those injured is of secondary importance. Suffering caused by conflict, injury or infectious disease only indicates that a curse is working and best not to be interfered with.

• Although legal and cultural interventions occur when conflict, disease, or accidents happen, those charged with responsibility in these cases are most interested in reinforcing honor and shame, not justice. Police, elders, judges, and sorcerers earn their living and honor through their manner of interventions, be it for good or evil.

In Catel, a village of about one hundred households, I could go down every pathway, visit every household, and in each one find people living lives dominated by tragedy, pain, abuse, suffering, brokenness, fear, conflict, exploitation, and death similar to those highlighted in Sabado's story. Relationships and actions growing out of loving care, community, compassion, peacemaking, and the dignity of persons are the rare exception rather than the rule.

This does not mean that God in his grace and goodness is not present in this setting. God's mercy, kindness, provision and healing are evident in spite of the marring and degradation of his creation. The problem is that God is not worshipped and his goodness is not recognized.

Satan and his minions are the primary power brokers and the recipients of people's adoration and supplications. For most people, God seems far away, mysterious and uninvolved; Satan is close, ever present, posing as a helper, and ready to use people for his destructive objectives.

How Did Things Ever Get This Bad?

From the day I arrived in West Africa in January 2000 and came face to face with this shocking depth and pervasiveness of human misery, my heart and soul cried out, "God, this can't be! This can't be! Here are beautiful people, created in your own image. How did things ever get this bad?"

I ask this question every time I see an unattended infant wallowing in the dirt and chewing on a filthy plastic bag, a woman who has been attacked coming to our clinic for wound care, men destroyed by alcohol dying in midlife, poor nutrition and no medical care, young men sitting day after day in idleness and without purpose in life.

I have spent years agonizing over these scenes of utter brokenness, tragedy, chaos, and death. I still search for answers.

In processing my question, I have often reflected on the words of the apostle Paul: "If you present yourselves to anyone as obedient slaves, you are slaves of the one whom you obey, either of sin, which leads to death, or of obedience, which leads to righteousness. . . . For just as you once presented your members as slaves to impurity and to lawlessness leading to more lawlessness, so now present your members as slaves to righteousness leading to sanctification" (Romans 6:13,19).

I have come to understand that evil spirits and evil powers are alive and well all over the world, but particularly here in

West Africa where nearly everyone has over-the-top faith in evil powers rather than in God, the Creator. Most people are openly in a faith/worship covenant with demonic forces for the power, direction, and authority they need for daily living.

When people "present" themselves to worship and give allegiance to physical objects of the creation and spiritual forces other than the Creator, greater and greater lawlessness will abound. Generation after generation here in West Africa has given faith, trust, and obedience to the demonic powers that perpetuate the fallenness of God's good creation. That explanation helps me to understand why things are this bad.

Spiritual Merchandisers

Every village has its spiritual marketplace, comprised of individuals who make their living pedaling powers and access to the unseen spiritual forces. In Catel, a community of fewer than 1,000 people, we had at least four such individuals, all with their own special spiritual gateway and merchandise. I knew it was not appropriate to approach these individuals and ask them to divulge their power sources and methods of interaction with the spirit world. But I did want to learn what I could about their trade.

A built-in obstacle to getting accurate information from these people is that their number one stock-in-trade is deception, sleight of hand, and naked untruth. Their enterprise is based on Satan, whom Jesus referred to as the father of lies.

Dubious though they may be, the stories of my visits with two of Catel's spiritual merchandisers provide some additional understanding of an animistic culture.

The first visit was with a friend/acquaintance whom I learned to know in my first days in Catel. He is in league with a female demon named Ancel. On weekends, to please her, he is trans-gendered into a female. His name changes from Louis to Toulai, and he goes around in a dress and headscarf. Numerous times he showed up at our clinic needing medicine for his ills and those of his family when his interventions did not work.

When I explained that I would like to ask him a few ques-tions about his "profession," he told me that when white people ask him to explain these things he requires them to first pay him with a ton of rice. The interview ended right there.

Next, I went down the road a couple hundred feet to see an-other purveyor of spiritual access. His name, Jean, signals some Christian connection. Most people of his tribe, the Mandiagos, have been baptized as infants into the Catholic Church. So his responses were naturally tinged with a guise of Christianity.

Because Jean was educated in Senegal and we could converse in French, it was easier to talk with him. He explained to me that his calling, what he termed a "traditional healer," came from God the Almighty, and he did only good and beneficial things for his clients. He claimed to have been born with the potential for being a traditional healer.

To become empowered for the tasks of a traditional healer, it was necessary for him to return to his ancestral village in the Mandiago tribal homeland about forty miles south of Catel. There he prepared festivities that included pouring out wine on the ground to draw in the spirits of the departed ancestors, along with the bodily presence of the village elders, various sorcerers, and many of his family and friends.

Animals were sacrificed and everyone prayed that he would receive the "gifting" that includes the ability to enlist ancestral spirits, prophecy, and clairvoyance. That done, he was equipped to help people with cures for illness, give direction in making decisions, place curses, undo curses, communicate with the ancestors, restore fertility and virility, extricate persons from legal quandaries, and assist with any other problems people might be facing.

Jean told me that he normally needs a night of sleep to come up with the solution to a client's dilemma since God nearly always reveals the solution and treatment process in dreams as he sleeps.

Most treatment plans include bathing in, drinking, or pouring out teas made from specific roots and tree bark particularly needed for the problem. He either gathers these materials himself in the wilds or purchases from herbalists.

He assured me that he does only good things, although others of his trade specialize in doing evil. If they have an evil heart, they have the ability to bring sickness, accidents, and even death to a client's enemies. Jean was hoping I would presume him not to be of that ilk, but I have reason to believe otherwise.

I was particularly interested in the belief that people can morph into either crocodiles or bobcats. Most people in Catel haven't the least doubt that some persons in the village turn into crocodiles or bobcats at night. That way they are able to attack their enemies and injure or even kill them. Bobcats are able to steal chickens, goats, and other small animals. They can also make currency out of mango leaves. Jean assured me that all this is true and happens frequently.

The question in front of each of us, including my friends in West Africa, is this: Whose team will I be on? Those of us who choose to be slaves of righteousness have become God's friends through the power of the Holy Spirit in our lives and in our communities of faith. As we live and move in the power of the Holy Spirit, God's kingdom is advanced into the realm of Satan, whose goal is to do everything possible to thwart people from entering into God's covenant of peace.

Several short-term groups join with locals in Catel for building projects. Here they are constructing the clinic building in 2009.

It is the task of missionaries, evangelists, and anyone who shares the good news of God's power over Satan to invite and encourage persons to leave the force field of Satan and join God's new people, who are being recreated and empowered through the faithfulness of Jesus Christ.

Demons in Daily Life

Westerners, from our rationalistic, enlightened worldview, are quick to say, "No way—demons and spiritual powers are only imaginary. They're not real. You can't see them. They don't occupy space and are not measureable." But in West Africa demons are real, especially in the lives of people who believe in them, worship them, and utilize their powers; they are an enormous presence to be reckoned with.

Daily life is ordered around the wishes and whims of demons and ancestral spirits. Ancestors and demons are consulted regarding many decisions:

This is a scene from a tribal initiation ceremony for young boys.
Some ceremonies involve demonic rituals, other activities are purely cultural. Christians are able to participate in a limited way but have the task of discerning where and when the rituals are to be avoided because of demonic content.

- When to plant crops— the farmer beseeches the ancestors to protect the crop and provide a bounteous harvest. The covenant with the spirits is sealed with pouring out a wine offering to the ancestor spirits

- How to start a business enterprise, whom to contact for securing required documentation, protection against curses and theft, and whom to trust and not trust as associates

- Where to find a wife who will be fertile, work hard, and bring honor to the family

- Where and when to build a house, protected from curses

- When to make a long trip, free from accident and accomplishing one's mission

Demons and ancestors can be manipulated to have power over others on your behalf. If you are suspicious of someone's designs or you think he may be doing something evil to you, you go straight to a sorcerer who can assist in summoning the power of a demon to help control the actions of your enemy, even kill him if necessary.

Practitioners of animism often are under contract with a specific demon. In exchange for the demon's power to make things happen in real life, the demon will sooner or later ask for a soul. The practitioner will tell the demon of a child he can take, and a neighborhood child dies without any known reason. Often a child who was healthy and active one day will be dead the next morning.

Other children contract illnesses that defy healing and they die an agonizing death over several days. In Guinea-Bissau, child mortality before the age of five is 20 percent. Contracts with demons are probably the cause of many of those deaths.

Age-group ties are very strong for boys who spend time together in bonding activities.

Preoccupation with the realm of evil spirits fosters the constant fear of what others might be plotting to do against you. A spirit of jealousy is ever present. A person who suspects someone is getting ahead financially may put a curse that destroys the other's source of income.

Trust levels are very low, even among family members. If a man has a business deal going on in the next town, he is careful not to tell anyone about it, including his wife, for fear his plans may be cursed. One who is sick doesn't want friends stopping by, for fear that visitors learning about his vulnerabilities and illness will put a death curse on him.

Animism destroys holistic social bonding and social responsibility. Parents are unable to show affection and support for their children because that might encourage them to advance ahead of their age mates. It prevents people from developing the trust in others so necessary for personal and corporate psychological well-being.

It also impedes economic development and binds people deeper into poverty. It stymies mutuality between married couples and mars other levels of familial solidarity. Animism is a tangled web of lies upon lies creating almost insurmountable barriers to progress and development.

Why does animism have such far-reaching social and economic consequences? Why does it wield so much power over so many aspects of human endeavor? It's because West African animism is the Vatican of Satanism. It's the devil's terrestrial homeland. Everything Satan desires is contrary to God's shalom and wholeness. And all of it is showcased in West Africa.

Animism in Action

Most animistic people believe sickness and accidents are the result of the intervention of a disturbed ancestor or an enemy's curse. Therefore, it is more important to deal with the spiritual and demonic powers that caused the illness than to treat it medically. The priority is to appease the disturbed ancestor or to counteract the curse from an enemy before even more damage.

As a result, there are many premature deaths, especially among children, because of not seeking medical care for easily treatable illnesses. Children are particularly vulnerable in this culture for many reasons, including the lack of basic home safety, lack of essential parenting skills, and the low value placed on children during their first ten years. Add to these factors the practice of not seeking medical care for treatable injury or illness, and Wilboy's story becomes possible.

Wilboy was a three-year-old girl from the village of Bandera, only a mile from the mission center in Catel. One early February afternoon a woman appeared at our gate, frantically telling us about Wilboy, who had been severely burned the previous day, and begging us to come tend to her.

Our medics, Terianne and Sean, quickly prepared their medical backpacks, and we set off on bicycles to Bandera. We found the house with a group of people gathered around the veranda, solemnly waiting for Wilboy's end and for the funeral festivities to begin. The child had burns over 40 percent of her body. Wilboy's distraught caregiver was on the ground rolling in the dirt and crying. The child's parents were not in the village.

The accident happened when the "auntie" left the compound to fetch water. Wilboy was left playing by herself in the yard along with a kettle of water perched on the three-stone fire pit. No one was there to watch Wilboy, and she got into the fire.

Now, more than 24 hours later, we had been summoned to help. We offered to take Wilboy to the hospital ten miles away, but no one showed any interest, even when we said she would probably die without prompt attention. We sensed the villagers preferred that we not intervene. Our medics noted that her lungs were filling with fluid, she was severely dehydrated, and she was in and out of consciousness.

The next morning Sean and Terianne went back to Bandera with dressings, an IV, and medicine to make Wilboy more comfortable. This time the folks at the house were open to intervention, and with a few days of diligent care on the part of our medics, Wilboy had passed a crisis and was showing some hope for survival.

As the medics made several additional visits, the family became interested in seeing Wilboy recover. Both her parents eventually showed up, and three days later they were ready to send her to the hospital. We took her to the closest facility, about ten miles away in the town of Sao Domingoes.

After two days there, the medical staff decided her condition was beyond what they were able to cope with, and they transferred her to the largest medical center in the country: the Simon Mendes Hospital in Bissau, the capital city. Sean and Terianne rode in the ambulance with Wilboy during the 50-mile trip to the hospital.

The nurse in charge of the ward was so impressed by the spirit and compassion of our medics that he got into the act as well, going out of his way to give special care to Wilboy. It looked like she would recover. But three weeks into her recovery, we got word from the hospital that she had died.

We don't know what happened to reverse the recovery. We only knew that now she was in the arms of Jesus.

The news was tough on Terianne and Sean. They had invested so much. People around the globe were praying for Wilboy, and it seemed only right that she could live a normal life even with the loss of fingers on her left hand. Moreover, her injury had appeared to be a way of reaching her family with the love of Christ. When the family witnessed the compassion Sean and Terianne poured into Wilboy, they too began to believe God was truly at work in healing Wilboy.

As expatriate missionaries living in a culture vastly different from ours, we struggled to make sense of the suffering of the little ones, the most innocent, the most vulnerable. The protection, care, and well-being of the little ones are not just part of the cultural baggage we bring along to the mission field. Our motivation comes from a source much higher than our culture; the words and example of Jesus inform our compassion and ministry for the little ones.

God is good, loving, and righteous. He is eternal, without beginning or end. Therefore goodness, love, righteousness and all his other attributes are from eternity past and will continue uninterrupted through eternity future.

Evil, on the other hand, is the interloper, but it is only provisional and time-bound. History is that blink of eternity in which God deals with evil and makes an end of it. Evil does not exist as an entity in its own right; it is only a perversion of the eternal good.

The qualities of evil are always nothing but untruth, deceit, and destruction. Evil's goal is to create division and enable rebellion against God's design for his creation. Evil flourishes in the context of darkness, ignorance, misery, poverty, and broken relationships. Mankind, living by the flesh, puts self and selfish ambition at the center of worship; therefore people become easy prey for Satan because he offers power over creation through exploitation and greed.

African Spirituality

In the Western mind, spirit-beings are the stuff of folklore and fairy tales. They exist only in the unhinged imagination. Not so in Africa. Spirit-beings, demons good and bad, and ancestors are as real and present as your two-year-old daughter or the tree beside the house. They hang around your veranda and mostly stay close to the front door. When you enter your house you need to acknowledge these unseen creatures. They attend every transaction of the day: your visit with a neighbor, the crops in your garden, the activities of your pregnant wife and the feeling that an insect is walking around inside your body.

I have a friend, who is now a pastor, who before his conversion wanted to secure a high position in the Senegal government. At the end of his high school education, when he was still an animist, he travelled into Guinea-Bissau to consult with a sorcerer on how he could use spiritual powers to obtain the desired appointment. He had full faith in the sorcerer's power because, just a few years prior to this, he had been through his tribal initiation ceremonies that involved a blood-letting pact with Satan, affording him access to satanic powers. This particular sorcerer was known far and wide as one who could empower career advancement. When my friend went to the sorcerer, he took with him two pullets before they had begun producing eggs.

The sorcerer killed the pullets and removed their intestines. After carefully examining the intestines, the sorcerer said, "Yes, you will be able to get a governmental appointment." He gave my friend a small goat horn instructing him to put the horn under his mattress; but every day he was to get it out and pour on a spoonful of wine.

My friend faithfully carried out the daily libation, but no government job ever came along. Soon after that he was converted and following Christ, totally renouncing any connection with occultic powers.

Now fast forward ten years, and he is attending a large convocation of West African pastors and church leaders at an upscale venue in Dakar sponsored by an internationally famous evangelist. Following a powerful message on what the Holy Spirit is able to do, the evangelist walked around the aisles, waving his jacket at rows of attendees, and scores of them fell over into a spiritual trance.

At the same crusade, my friend attended a special prayer session. Here those seeking answers to prayer lined up in one of three rows, assembly-line fashion. Row one was for those wanting to travel to the U.S. or Europe. Row two was for those wanting a spouse. Row three was for those wanting God to multiply their financial assets. Each row required one to drop an offering into the coffer just before getting a thumb print of holy oil on the forehead and a prayer by the pastor in charge of that particular line.

Going to the U. S. and getting a spouse required a donation of at least $40, while having your finances multiply had no set cost since the more you gave, the more the Lord would multiply. Most people held their offering in their hand so that everyone could see how much they gave. Some were brandishing several hundred dollars.

My pastor friend didn't participate, but he was an observer to the show. His conclusion was that his experience with the sorcerer was essentially the same as what was happening at the Christian crusade. It was little more than an attempt to use spiritual forces to further one's personal, carnal agenda, on the part of both the supplicant and the spiritual merchandiser.

In much of Africa, this is the sum and substance of "church," spiritual manipulation behind a thinly disguised Christian façade, with all prayers ending with a forceful, "In the name of Jesus."

When I facilitate at seminars in West Africa, I listen to many such stories, all with a ring similar to what one reads in Acts 8:9-24 (Simon, the magician); in Acts13:8-11 (Elymas, the magician) and in Acts 19:13-20 (the seven sons of Sceva).

Spiritual merchandisers nearly always have a tangible object or fetish that embodies and conveys the spiritual power; for example, holy water with dissolved ink from Koranic verses, prayer beads, animal parts, scarves and teas. A seminar participant from Kenya told me of a mega church in Nairobi where the fetish was a small broom. The lead pastor had purchased a container with thousands of these small whisk brooms which he had anointed with power to sweep evil out of one's life and house. Anyone who had financial problems, health problems or a troublesome in-law could simply purchase the broom and literally sweep the hassles out of his life.

Once the practitioner had sold all the brooms, he packed up and disappeared.

Why do Africans easily get on board with spiritual powers and fetishes?

Tears of Compassion

When Christians, whether African or from outside of Africa, get a good picture of what is happening here in West Africa in terms of who is in control of the spiritual and physical well-being of these people, and daily confront the devastation and carnage of Satan's power, their hearts and spirits respond very similarly to the way Jesus reacted when he came to live among his people.

Within days of the end of his earthly life, as Jesus was approaching Jerusalem for the last time, Luke records that "when

he drew near and saw the city, he wept over it, saying, 'Would that you, even you, had known on this day the things that make for peace! But now they are hidden from your eyes.'"

This little boy sits in a typical classroom. Most schools are quite primitive. In many villages the literacy rate is less than 20% because of the lack of educational opportunities.

Time and time again as I see with my eyes and contemplate in my spirit the lostness and wretchedness of God's creation and his people in

West Africa, I weep. I weep because I know that Jesus is also here weeping. His words are the same today as they were then: "Would that you, even you, had known on this day the things that make for peace! But now they are hidden from your eyes."

Another incident from the life of Jesus that compels the missionary in the West Africa setting is found in the Gospel of Matthew: "Jesus went throughout all the cities and villages, teaching in their synagogues and proclaiming the gospel of the kingdom and healing every disease and every affliction. When he saw the crowds, he had compassion for them, because they were harassed and helpless, like sheep without a shepherd. Then he said to his disciples, 'The harvest is plentiful, but the laborers are few; therefore pray earnestly to the Lord of the harvest to send out laborers into his harvest.'"

Jesus' reaction to the human situation is one of compassion. He created us and knows our need to be shepherded and cared for spiritually and physically. When he sees his creation lost and helpless, far from the wholeness he created us to enjoy, he is moved to great compassion, praying that laborers will be sent out to bring shalom to his sheep.

That's what being a missionary is all about. We want to open doors for people, encouraging them to leave their brokenness and enter into the way of peace and joy which our Father God has created us to enjoy.

We are not here to impose a foreign culture on the locals; we have no desire or reason to destroy their culture and way of life. We are simply offering God's salvation, which will transform individuals and communities through friendship with God. As new believers begin to experience the joy, forgiveness, and peace of life in his kingdom, they begin to find ways to transform their culture so that the culture reflects the will of God for his people.

Real Life Transformations

We have seen the new believers in Catel transforming both their culture and their individual lives in several ways:

- Fathers have begun to help their wives with child care and household tasks.

- Men are becoming accustomed to regular work schedules.

- Spousal fidelity is becoming accepted as the norm.

- Parents are teaching their children how to settle arguments peacefully instead of violently.

- There is less violence in family relationships, between men and women and between parents and their children.

- Families are making an effort to increase household cleanliness to prevent infectious diseases.

- Drunkenness has diminished; there is less violence and anti-social behavior.

- Families are preparing nutritionally better-balanced meals.

- People gather to worship God alone; witchcraft is no longer needed, since they are in God's care.

- The amount of stealing, deception, and lying has decreased. Fear levels are down; trust levels are up.

- There is greater commitment to literacy.

- Compassionate relationships are on the rise.

- Believers take the initiative in community peacemaking.

- Awareness of health and physical well-being issues has increased.

- People seek medical treatment for injuries and diseases.

- A growing concern for creation care is evident, especially in farming practices.

- Compassionate care is being offered to those who are suffering and discouraged by life's hardships. Shaming and abuse are being replaced by mercy and healing.

- Christians are inviting their friends and family to begin to experience God's love and light. They freely share the Good News in a non-coercive, invitational manner. When transformation is observed in the lives of family members who have become believers, others are soon open to becoming part of the good things they observe in the believers.

- Believers boldly confront evil around them and are prepared to suffer and sacrifice with Christ to enable others to experience the salvation and restoration God offers to all.

Conversion as Reorientation

To those who denigrate missionaries as destroyers of culture, I would ask several questions: Do you have a problem with people making the sorts of cultural transformations noted above, all of which enhance human dignity? Is it not normal for people to seek better living standards? Would you stand in the way of the humanization of the world's marginalized?

In West Africa there is absolutely only one way to break free from the bondage of poverty and the power of satanic lies that block Africans from realizing life as God created it to be enjoyed—the appropriation, corporately and individually, of the power of the resurrected Christ and his defeat of Satan in the cosmic battle over evil.

Children between the ages of 3-8 typically have a diet mostly of rice. They are not technically malnourished but the high carbohydrate diet causes stunting in growth.

Disbarring Africans from knowing liberation from the terrors of animism that I have portrayed in this chapter has got to be imperialism at its worst. Christianity doesn't destroy culture; it frees individuals and communities to experience their culture in ways that dignify and humanize people and honor our creator God.

Another way of thinking about what happens when a West African moves out of animism into New Testament faith in Christ is to think of his conversion as cultural reorientation. This happens as the missionary directs the seeker's attention to the ways he is already experiencing God in his cultural/geographic setting. God is already here in his grace, providence, and power, but the average West African is under such a heavy tangle of satanic lies that he is unable to see God's presence.

For example, my friends in Catel are all subsistence farmers; they live very close to the soil and are directly dependent on the land for their survival. They are highly dependent on the rainy season/dry season weather cycle and the fruition of various crops as they move through the annual rhythm of planting, growth, and harvest. Three crops are cultivated and harvested during the year: peanuts, cashews, and mangos. Between harvests of these crops, the margin between life and disaster becomes really narrow.

But moving towards life in Christ begins to radically change the equation. In what ways does becoming a Christian potentially reorient the life of a subsistence farmer?

- He discovers that it is God, not Satan, who has created and sustains life. God is in charge of the cycles of nature and has ordained ways of caring for the soil to restore fertility and make it more productive. He discovers that the ancestral spirits, enemy curses, and the neighborhood sorcerer actually have no power over nature when he belongs to the community of faith in Christ.

- He begins to learn about agronomy, soil structure, composting, biological control of pests, and the importance of mulch and crop rotation.

- He begins to understand the nutritional needs of his family and why it is important to farm year-round to grow a wide variety of fruits and vegetables.

Getting the picture of cultural reorientation? Transformation of every aspect of the social and cultural life of West Africa—gender relations, family life, childrearing, village politics, health and hygiene, formal education—could be described as reorientation according to God's design. Culture is critiqued by godly standards and brought back into God's original harmonious design. Nothing in the culture that builds human dignity and shalom is lost.

Christian missionaries understand this transformation and reorientation as the "in-breaking" of the kingdom of God. Satanic destruction and chaos are pushed back as God's kingdom comes and his will is done on earth, in West Africa and elsewhere, as it is in heaven.

Spiritual Warfare

"Spiritual warfare" is anything we do through prayer, proclamation, or loving deeds that opens windows for persons, enabling them to see and experience the present kingdom of God. Spiritual warfare encourages, persuades, and empowers people to accept and appropriate Christ's defeat of Satan, already accomplished through his faithfulness in life, death, and glorious resurrection.

Spiritual warfare invites and persuades people to make the victory of Christ over Satan a reality in their hearts and minds. It encourages persons to begin to experience the difference the reign of God makes in their relationship to everything else in his creation. Godly qualities such as love, light, truth, harmony, and peace will become the garden in which our relationships will flourish as satanic footholds are banished from our lives and communities.

The gospel narratives portray Jesus as battling spiritually with demons that are in possession of individuals as well as with structural evil manifested in abuse of power by social, religious, and political institutions. Jesus establishes a new community of people with relationships based on peace, nonviolence, and suffering love.

In the new, alternate community of Christ there is loving, caring service for each other because we see others as created in the image of God. In the community of Christ, our goal is to be servants, not masters; we seek to serve rather than to be served.

God's plan for us is healing, peace, wholeness, contentment, adequate provision, and loving relationships. To bring us into these, he offers a covenanted relationship backed up by his self-sacrificing, unconditional love. Moreover, he enables our faithfulness to his covenant by adopting us as his children and recreating his righteous image and presence within us, both at the personal and community level.

God's plan for the redemption of mankind and all of creation has been assured through the coming of Jesus, who is God in flesh, to live among us. Jesus was the utterly faithful second Adam, the first to become all that the Father God desires for all of his creation. In his faithful obedience to God, his death and glorious resurrection, Jesus became a first fruit of God's design for each and every one of us.

Jesus came as a divine warrior sent to do battle with the "powers," not to "wrestle against flesh and blood, but against the rulers, against the authorities, against the cosmic powers over this present darkness, against the spiritual forces of evil in the heavenly places" (Ephesians 6:12).

Spiritual warfare at the cosmic level is done, finished and over. God, through the faithfulness of his Son Jesus Christ, has defeated Satan and his kingdom of death and darkness. We conclude with the testimony of Sieaka, a new believer who lives life in the reality of the victory of Christ over the satanic forces.

At the time of this story Sieaka had been participating in our church for less than a year. He is from the Mandiago tribe and grew up in a village near Catel. He initially attended church to ask for physical healing after ministrations of the witch doctors proved useless. Sieaka is in his late thirties and had been experiencing various long-term illnesses. He had previously participated in a Catholic church and with the New Apostolic. Neither of these church experiences resulted in spiritual growth or transformation nor did he realize physical healing.

When he came to Catel Mennonite and asked us to pray for his healing, he was set free from various physical afflictions. Since then he has become an eager disciple of Jesus and actively participates in the program, sharing his faith with many others and offering his gifts of wisdom and stability to the community.

In the middle of a June night in 2012, his mother was awakened by the incessant barking of their dog. She did some checking in the area in front of the house and was able to see that some of their cows, tethered for the night in the dooryard, were missing. Before they could get the search underway, two of the cows had already wandered back, but two were missing.

Cattle thievery is common in this country and probably goes back to a long raiding tradition between villages and tribes. Successful thievery is considered a mark of a brave, successful man. In stealing one puts his life on the line because if he is caught in the act he can be shot with no questions asked. If he makes good on the thievery, he is a hero.

This incident was one of two attempts by thieves to steal Sieaka's cows. The thieves previously were successful in getting away with two cows, loading them into a transport van and fleeing. Now they had returned.

On this second incident of thievery, Sieaka left the house to start the search for the cows, taking a gun with him. He made a note to himself, however, that he was to use it to scare off the thieves, not to injure or kill them. As a new Christian, he says, he knew it would not be right for him to end the life of another. Only God has the power to do that.

Finally he came to a clearing just off the highway where the thieves were attempting to force two cows into the van. Sieaka shot his gun into the air, causing the thieves to flee for their lives. They fled on foot leaving behind the vehicle as prima fascia evidence. The police located the vehicle owner in a town fifty miles away, and through Sieaka they were able to identify the thieves.

There are two systems of justice in this country to deal with an incident like this. One is to organize friends and neighbors to go after the thieves and mete out a punishment that far outweighs the damages done, possibly even killing them. The other system is to turn the prosecution over to the police and the regional courts.

In this case, because the police were already involved, the second option was followed. But because the system is so fraught with corruption, the guilty are seldom punished other than being detained in jail a few days.

Despite the injustice done him in the loss of his cows and the ineptness of the judicial system, Sieaka has come to a place of peace about it. He has sensed God's care throughout this difficult time. He has completely turned the situation over to the justice of God. He is at peace that God's justice will, in the end, prevail.

As I consider stories of my friends such as Sieaka and I see the power of the Spirit of Jesus at work in their lives, I ponder anew the mystery of Christ's call to follow him in life and how individuals turn towards Jesus to begin the journey with him.

When Sieaka responded positively to Jesus' call, he knew almost nothing about Jesus. He knew only about Jesus' power to heal and make things better. He had never heard of the rapture, inerrancy of Scripture, the virgin birth nor any of the other hallmark Christian doctrines, nor was he able to give an explanation as to how or why Jesus is the healer. He only knew enough about this man to reach out to the one who has the power to deliver from evil and sickness. I think of how close this is to the way Jesus interacted with people while he was here in his earthly ministry. People saw him as a prophet, a man with God's power to make things right.

Once Jesus has their attention and they are able to get beyond the jolt of the sign he invites them to come, be part of his new community of faith, a new people of God who are citizens of another kingdom. Through the power of the Spirit he begins to transform them into the new creation that God originally intended for each of us.

Evangelism and mission viewed through this lens is a liberating experience, even for the missionary. The missionary community is a group of Jesus followers who are a bit further along in their journey and are eager to include new seekers. They are open to freely walk along side persons upon whom the light is just now breaking; not domineering, coercing, or threatening, just being there in a loving, supportive and encouraging way as the Spirit does his astonishing re-creation. (With this definition of missionary, even I can be one!)

The missionary doesn't try to play God even though God has "seated us with him in the heavenly places in Christ Jesus" (Ephesians 2:6), and has given us all power. The missionary is a servant willing to risk pain, inconvenience, even life itself just to help seekers to see, experience and know Messiah Jesus.

It's a win/win. Sieaka has decided to follow a new master; the missionaries have once again been faithful bearers of the good news of God's kingdom.

Chapter 5

The Spiritual Itinerary

Anyone listening to the faith journey stories of first-generation Christians in West Africa soon picks up common characteristics of life during their pre-Christian years: We used to go to the sacred tree, get advice from the witchdoctor, wear amulets for protection from attacks to harm us, pour libations out to the ancestors, talk to the spirits around our house, place curses of vengeance, do pre-planting and post-harvest rituals, help our family members move through death into life in the next world, watch for signs of impending tragedy, make pacts with demonic powers and many more. All these activities were their ways of dealing and reckoning with the ever present, nearby spiritual powers sharing space with mortals.

Moving from solid, all-out animism "until we all attain to the unity of the faith and of the knowledge of the Son of God, to mature manhood, to the measure of the stature of the fullness of Christ" (Ephesians 4:13), requires a special faith itinerary all its own. (Note: Credit for some of the comments about the faith itinerary that follow belongs to David A. Shank, author of *Missions from the Margins*). The journey usually requires years of discipling, encouragement, and nurture, very different from the typical North American notion of just-add-water-and stir instant Christians.

American missionaries going out to "evangelize in the villages" in West Africa is a charade more for the benefit of the sending congregation than for the African animist. The missionary sends back glowing reports of decisions for Christ and baptisms. Mission accomplished! Missionaries continue to maintain this 19th century model because it is what mission boards and their supporting constituents expect of them. It's what raises the bucks to perpetuate the illusion of evangelism.

My friend Sherif is a more realistic example of the journey of conversion from animism to a fully thriving disciple of Christ. He was born in the village of Karounate near where the Casamance River empties into the Atlantic, perhaps 75 miles northwest of our mission in Guinea-Bissau. Sherif told me about growing up in a West Africa animistic village and his faith itinerary into Christ.

Like all babies in the village, he was born out in the forest in a birthing hut with the assistance of a mid-wife friend of his mother. No men were present, not even the father. Six days after birth, the newborn was committed to a spirit-being as a guide throughout his years and even into the next life. Sherif's mother was from the family of the head fetisher for Karounate, known as one of the most powerful fetishes in the region. Sherif grew up heavily under the influence of witchcraft and demonic powers.

Sherif's village, like all the neighboring villages, had its own sorcerer who maintained a host of power secrets of that particular village's spirit beings. The sorcerer, commonly known as the fetisher, roughly equivalent to a priest, maintains a sacred site in the forest where he conducts occultic séances and consults the spirits on behalf of the villagers. The fetisher's main functions are to manipulate spiritual powers, provide guidance in decision making and invoke vengeance curses for the villagers. All interactions with the spirits must be paid for by sacrifices of animals and wine. Failure to provide the required sacrifice to the spirit will result in instant death.

These young men have spent several weeks in the forest as part of the tribal initiation rituals. Christians do not participate in this part of the initiation rites because demonic pacts are made during the forest ceremonies.

The sacred forest is a site no one visits except in the presence of the fetisher. To go there without him means certain death. The sacred forest is a focal point in the initiation rites for boys entering adulthood and into the tribe. It is here they learn the clan's power secrets and how to manipulate the spirit beings living among them in the village. Women are not allowed in the sacred forest precincts because they are at risk of divulging the village power secrets to families in other villages.

The spirit-being in Karounate had many rules on what one does and does not do in his presence within the sacred forest. One of the spirit's injunctions was that the spirit could not tolerate talk of polygamy within the sacred forest. One day Sherif's uncle made the mistake of bringing up the subject of polygamy, and the very next day he fell to his death from a palm tree when his climbing harness mysteriously severed.

Karounate's location, not far from the tidal Casamance river, makes fishing a significant income source. Sherif's house had a dried fish storage area that was protected by a snake. The family was able to manage the snake through spirit powers, but a thief would be bitten by the snake and soon die. Snakes are a potent power source of spiritual control.

No one from outside the village was allowed to eat the fruit from trees on land owned by the villagers. The fruit trees were protected by a curse; any outsider eating the fruit would soon get sick and die. One time there was a wedding in the village, and several of the guests ate the fruit; within three days some of them became ill and died.

Not long after Sherif grew up and left Karounate to live in Ziguinchor, the head fetisher died. Even now, many years after his death, no one has been found to take his place because the fetish is so strong no one is capable of managing it.

After moving to Ziguinchor, as a young man, Sherif began attending an evangelical church and was converted. That is to say, he prayed the sinner's prayer and accepted Jesus into his heart following the evangelical routines for "getting saved." And he was baptized. However, he wasn't really saved from anything. He still lived in fear of demonic powers, still secretly kept some of his personal fetishes and he was unable to understand anything he read in the Bible—this despite his regular attendance at worship services, Bible studies and seminars. He kept up this Christian masquerade for nineteen years!

Then one day he attended a seminar in Dakar, and the instructor told the students to begin praying for their unbelieving family members. Somehow through that experience, he saw a curtain being lifted off his mind, and the love, the light and the Spirit of God simply flooded his heart and soul. He began weeping, and for several days he could only weep. Even the seminar instructor couldn't figure out what was going on with him. But Sherif knew what was happening: he was finally transitioning into a bona fide disciple of Jesus.

Since that day he easily understands his Bible reading, enjoys Bible studies, and is in constant awareness of God's presence and power in his life. He is an elder in one of the evangelical congregations of Ziguinchor. Although he has long since burned his fetish items, he still senses tension with his family; they consider him disloyal to the family and clan. He visits his family in Karounate but refuses to spend a night in the village.

For people like Sherif who have spent their growing up years in this heavily animistic culture, it is completely unrealistic to think all this animistic baggage will suddenly vanish when someone goes through the four spiritual laws and repeats the sinner's prayer. It requires a journey of several years involving numerous stages of transitioning.

An aside: The reason we have instant conversions in America is essentially the same. Conversion is understood as a spiritual transaction somewhere up in heaven whereby one is declared righteous and real life transitions are rare.

The task of the West African missionary, whether or not he is cross-cultural or a native African, is to nurture seekers in their transition from animistic spirituality into becoming a disciple of Jesus. The missionary teaches, encourages, nurtures and challenges seekers along the pathway of faithfulness, openness and obedience to Messiah Jesus. The missionary opens windows for seekers as they move towards full participation and faithfulness to the incarnate Word and the kingdom of God.

My task in writing this book has been to monitor how the Mennonite mission team has performed in the ministry of discipling people for Jesus during our pioneer years. As I have interviewed believers, I have heard common refrains as people told their stories of how they moved out of animism and began the journey of discipleship with Jesus.

One observation was shared by nearly everyone I talked with: "When I began attending services and Bible studies at the Mennonite Church, I began to understand the Bible; it all started making sense. I had heard sermons, been through catechism, and been in other settings of training, but somehow nothing sort of jelled and came together as a unified picture of God's overall salvation for his creation and what he was calling me to do and become. But as I attended Bible studies, listened to the preaching and participated in Catel Mennonite, I caught a vision of how God was calling me and everyone into a new life in his family."

After hearing several believers saying essentially this same thing, I began to ask questions. What are we doing that is right? What is there about our ministry and teaching program that helps people successfully move into a discipleship relation with Jesus? Whatever we were doing we need to keep doing it! As I put this question to church members, I got these answers:

1. You came to live among us for the long term, shared life with us even to the point of suffering with the pain of our darkness and poverty.

2. You came to accept us and love us even before we were ready to become part of the community of faith. You understood and sympathized with us in our spiritual darkness and lostness without condemning us. You valued us as people despite our ignorance.

3. Your way of living demonstrated what you were teaching us. Others taught how things like witchcraft and immoral living are not the way of Jesus, but freedom from evil was readily evident in your lives.

4. Following teaching and preaching, you always listened to our questions and confusion, helping us to a place of clarity and understanding of the Bible.

5. You were not expecting us to memorize a catechism or embrace a particular system of theology. Your goal was to help us get on board with God's kingdom and his will for our lives; simply becoming a disciple of Jesus. You had high expectations of us, but you also allowed us time and space to get there.

6. You encouraged us to listen not just to what you had to say, but also listen to our brothers and sisters as they processed what it means to be a disciple of Jesus. Hearing other's struggles allowed us to grow both personally and into a family of faith.

In my reading I came across the three B's of forming and drawing seekers into the community of Christ: believing, belonging and becoming. As people move in the direction of Jesus, there is an animated interplay of these three, and each needs to be present. One need not put one ahead of the other or somehow prioritize them, but simply encourage them to flourish as the wind of the Spirit blows. The results will be a joy to behold.

Let's look at some of the steps in the itinerary as one moves from animism to becoming a disciple of Jesus and note how the missionary is a facilitator in helping persons move through the process.

Some Basic Assumptions

1. All of us, African, European or whoever, are confronted with the gracious offer of right relationship with God, our Father/ Creator.

2. Because of being created in his image, there is the potential for a longing within everyone to come back, to find and know God and to be in solidarity with him and his divine will.

3. Movement back to God is an incremental, gradual process; a passage of somewhat defined stages of spiritual discovery, discernment and appropriation. The process needs to be on both a personal level and in the communitarian, people of God, context.

4. The missionary mandate to make disciples kicks in even at an early stage of one's relationship/discipleship with Jesus. Persons in the early stages of discovering their joy and freedom in Christ are among those most eager to share the Good News with their families, friends, neighbors and even cross-culturally.

Other Considerations

Thus, all Christians and would-be believers find themselves somewhere along the way on a track that recreates lives, hearts and minds into what God designed us to be; the healing of what has been marred by sin. How we move along that continuum is conditioned by our theological heritage and how the New Testament teachings are handed on to us through preaching, worship forms, religious institutions, traditions, rituals and doctrinal understandings. Each stage along the way should open up new vistas for our spiritual development and create a desire to mature.

Some church communities and individuals can become blocked or locked into one particular stage of spiritual development because of the way biblical truth is ignored, excluded, distorted or disobeyed.

The typical itinerary suggests nothing about the length of time a person or group may spend in a given stage of spiritual development. Illumination, with commitment, may happen rapidly or it can be delayed. But each time new understandings and illumination occur, based on previous experience, and followed by commitment, there is spiritual growth.

An example of arrested spiritual development has been cited by African theologians who note that some Western missionaries have come to Africa with a moral code from a God whom the Africans hardly understood or trusted. As a result, some Christians spend the rest of their lives trying to obey God and please the missionaries or pastors, only to fail at every turn. Where the gospel is presented as a new law, a legalistic Christianity results, and the whole point of a gracious redemption is missed.

As an alternative to this scenario, here in Guinea-Bissau we have first presented Jesus as God's Messiah of grace, acceptance, love, transformation and discipleship. Instead of starting in Genesis 1-3 with the fall and how all that got worked through, we start with the stories of One who was sent by God to show us how he created us to live. Through the work of the Holy Spirit, he invites us to become part of God's new people. Such an approach, will in the end, produce morally upright believers, transformed from the inside out, empowered by the Holy Spirit.

Jesus becomes the norm for what life is like in God's kingdom, a present reality as his will is being done here in Guinea-Bissau, the way it is done in heaven. The kingdom of God gateway is the confession that Jesus Christ is indeed God's Messiah. This confession authenticates itself in submission and obedience to the Lordship of Jesus in daily life, actions, attitudes and relationships.

In some Christian persuasions the gateway confession is, "Jesus died on the cross to take away my sins and guilt so I will be able to spend eternity with God in Heaven." In West Africa, many preachers feel compelled to somehow include this salvation formula into every message. This is a confession that shortchanges, trivializes and dishonors the all-inclusive faithfulness and salvation of Messiah Jesus; and it is an unstable foundation for spiritual development. This type of conversion, like a worn-out car, requires constant maintenance to keep it going. One is constantly reminded of shortcomings that jeopardize his eternal destiny.

With these understandings, we can put together some of the steps in the progression of faith development as it moves from traditional West African animism towards New Testament faith.

First we make a comparison of spiritual values in these two faith systems.

African Traditional Religion vs. New Testament Faith

The spirits of the ancestors hold sway over the living. There is a constant need to be cognizant of wishes, needs and well-being of the ancestors.

Although thankful for faithful ancestors, we live in the present and coming kingdom of God.

Creator, all powerful God is unquestionably there but is scarcely known. He is regularly invoked but remains distant and uninvolved.

Faith commitment is made to the Redeemer God revealed in Messiah Jesus.

The most important social framework is the tribe, family and village. They establish right vs. wrong and are the locus of power and loyalty.

Social framework is the church, the people of God. Membership is based on a freewill, adult decision.

Life is fearful, controlled by amulets and fetishes, and spiritual rituals.

Life is service, justice, peace, holiness, freedom in Christ and life in the Spirit.

Life values are to attain and maintain power, prosperity, posterity and honor.

God's required righteousness is fulfilled as one follows Jesus and lives by the Spirit. There is loving obedience, discipleship and full participation in God's kingdom now.

Social control is realized through fear, shame, curses, taboos and ceremonies. Persons straying outside this fence are at least shamed and may risk persecution and death.

Satan and demonic forces are vanquished through faithfulness to Christ, prayer, exorcism and fellowship in the community of Christ.

Good spirits, properly appeased, bring safety, health, blessing and prosperity.

The church is the community of gifts, spiritual discernment, vision.

Evil spirits can be used to control others and punish enemies.

Christians experience providential intervention by God and mutual aid in community.

The marabou and jumbakuse are diviners who offer counsel, design plans for success and vengeance, mediate curses, sell herbals, create protective amulets and fetishes, and preside over spiritual rituals.

Resurrection and assurance of future life with God and his redeemed creation are promised.

Progressive Stages of Faith Transformation

In the journey from animism to fullness in Christ, the believer must pass through numerous stages of development and maturation of faith and faithfulness. These transitions call for spiritual guidance graced by patience, forgiveness, positive reinforcement and undying hope.

1. Conversion is from belief in multiple capricious spiritual forces to faith in a single all-powerful Being who is active, faithful and close. The Father God becomes known through his acts of protection, healing, blessing and peace.

2. A period of struggle accompanies the abandoning of old sources of power and protection. Belief in the one true God is tested many times. One is not surprised when there are lapses of faithfulness.

3. The need to return evil for evil is abandoned. Understanding grows that vengeance belongs to the Lord and that ultimate power is in the cross, where good overcomes evil.

4. The will of God, the Bible itself and Christian symbols replace fetishes.

5. God is worshipped in the house of God, a specific building or place where Christians gather.

6. Pastors are needed to mediate God's power, expectations of the church and Christian discipline.

7. Personal responsibility before God and fellowmen is discovered gradually.

8. When others, especially family members, are not able to accept the gospel and abandon paganism, Christians feel disquiet and anguish.

9. Movement towards the grace of God enables the believer to live righteously before him, as revealed in the Second Adam example and teachings of Christ.

10. One learns what it means to live by the Spirit, and to exercise gifts granted by the Holy Spirit. Fruits of the Spirit become more obvious along with a growing sense of peace and assurance with God.

11. The body of disciples becomes the community of Christ. How the community develops and conducts itself becomes an eschatological sign of God's reign in the here and now. The community of Christ stands in direct opposition to the kingdom of Satan.

Other Markers and Mileposts

1. Deep concern about the next life becomes a deep concern for becoming the new creation now, and we focus on being a testimony for God's righteousness.

2. Attraction to the Old Testament moves toward a deepening appreciation for the New.

3. The significance of power signs gives way to the ministry and teaching of the Word.

4. Idol worship and sacred tree rituals are replaced by personal and corporate prayer.

5. The domination of shame as a social control is replaced by a sense of guilt at the violation of God's plan.

6. Periodic Holy Spirit interventions become the abiding presence of the Spirit of Christ.

Some Significant Flaws in Expatriate Missionary Strategy

1. Our agenda as expatriate missionaries has been influenced by Enlightenment rationalism, racism, and results-driveness more than we realize or care to admit. We need to repent from these and tell God we want to do mission the Jesus way.

2. Some of what we have accepted as good evangelistic strategy is arrogant, power driven and presumptuous and can retard or sidetrack the faith itinerary. Some Western missionaries appear to have borrowed pages from a U.S. Army battle strategy handbook: reconnaissance, strategic planning, move in, establish base, take command, execute plan, and move out. Mission accomplished.

3. We need to take our cues from what we already know about God's progressive revelation of himself in history as a model for persons individually and corporately. Sharing the gospel is not the overnight, once and done, surgically clean event we imagine it to be.

Faith Itinerary Servant-Facilitators

Two scriptures inform our role as we serve and guide people along their faith journey:

"That which is born of the flesh is flesh, and that which is born of the Spirit is spirit. Do not marvel that I said to you, 'You must be born again.' The wind blows where it wishes, and you hear its sound, but you do not know where it comes from or where it goes. So it is with everyone who is born of the Spirit" (John 3:6-8).

"...in humility count others more significant than yourselves. Let each of you look not only to his own interests, but also to the interests of others. Have this mind among yourselves, which is yours in Christ Jesus, who, though he was in the form of God, did not count equality with God a thing to be grasped, but made himself nothing, taking the form of a servant, being born in the likeness of men. And being found in human form, he humbled himself by becoming obedient to the point of death, even death on a cross" (Philippians 2:3-8).

Worldview Transformation

Just a short diversion here so we understand what is meant by worldview. Worldview is a collection of presuppositions of a people, collected and honed by generations as they seek to understand the nature of things and how life should be ordered.

Worldview attempts to answer essential question of existence such as these:

- Where did we come from; how did we get here?

- What should we be doing; what is right, good, and best?

- What are the actions we should take to attain our goals as a culture?

- What is true or false, good or bad, beautiful or ugly, forward or backward?

- Is our timeline linear or cyclical?

Worldview is a committed, fundamental orientation of the heart and spirit regarding the presuppositions which we hold about the basic construction of reality providing us the foundation on which "we live and move and have our being" to borrow the Apostle Paul's quote from a Greek poet.

During my first two years in Catel, Guinea-Bissau, as I learned more about the culture, I gradually began to assess the distance between God's moral truth as understood in the Bible and the Bissau worldview. I had no desire to help transform these people into a North American worldview, but their worldview was in great need of being critiqued by God's heart for his creation. Evangelism, the Good News of Jesus, is unapologetically worldview transformational and at the same time affirmative of things already in the culture that reflect the righteousness of the Creator.

Doing evangelism, church or theology in West Africa, or anywhere else in the world, will entail critical contextualization in which the culture is studied and understood by the missionaries together with local Christian leaders; then Scripture (that is, the truth and morality of the Bible), is used to evaluate and correct the culture and its worldview. These understandings are essential for worldview transformation which starts the day the pioneer missionary arrives on the scene and remains on-going in the life of the Christian community that has been established.

Helping believers to take ownership of critical contextualization is key. We help believers to understand God's vision for his people and all of creation, and then we engage them to evaluate their cultural practices in relation to God's vision. We have had animated discussions with spontaneous participation on gender relations, family life, sexuality, agriculture, health, non-violence, work, education and more. As the discerning community participates in the evaluation based on Bible understanding, the process of spiritual maturing moves forward.

Worldview transformation always has the goal to "Have this mind among yourselves, which is yours in Christ Jesus" (Philippians 2:5). And "we all, with unveiled face, beholding the glory of the Lord, are being transformed into the same image from one degree of glory to another. For this comes from the Lord who is the Spirit" (2 Corinthians 3:18).

Worldview Components Needing Critique

These are some of the major worldview components evident in Bissau culture that need transformation:

- A profound marginalization of women and children

- The easy disregard for civil society and individual rights

- The neglect of basic health care in favor of deadly voodoo

- Use of scarce financial resources to carry out animistic and ancestral ceremonies

- Levels of food production kept low because of the ignorance of creation care principles

- Brief life expectancy and high infant mortality fatalistically accepted, even valued

- Low self-esteem for being African

- Repayment of evil with evil; captivity to the cycle of increasing violence

- Controlling others through intimidation, prowess and fear

- Rampant sexual promiscuity

- Virtually no trust in communal, familial and political relations

A pioneer missionary's heart is often encouraged by this verse: "My little children, for whom I am again in the anguish of childbirth until Christ is formed in you!" (Galatians 4:19).

Chapter 6

The Gospel is Cross Cultural

In my years of preparation for a return to Africa the thought would occasionally flash through my mind: What if, when I finally arrive in Africa, the Africans do not accept me? What would I do then? Well, obviously, quite the opposite is reality; everywhere I go in Africa I have been so warmly received that now I have no intention of leaving.

We all have a kind of innate fear of cultures and places different from our own. A deep, intense fear is called xenophobia. Because that fear dominates many Americans, relatively few travel overseas, even for a vacation, let alone live abroad as a long-term missionary. Imagination can suggest all sorts of cultural barriers to leaving the homeland shores: Over there it's not safe, the food is bad, people aren't friendly, I will get sick, maybe even die, I can't speak the language, I need to stay here with my family and on and on.

In contrast, Jesus talks about leaving familiar territory for the sake of the kingdom as if it is the norm for anyone expecting to participate in God's kingdom, present and future: "Truly, I say to you, there is no one who has left house or wife or brothers or parents or children, for the sake of the kingdom of God, who will not receive many times more in this time, and in the age to come eternal life" (Luke 18:29).

The gospel of God's kingdom is, itself, a cross-cultural phenomenon. God's covenant with Abraham was a promise to bring blessing to all people groups through the descendents of Abraham. And the word of the prophets through the centuries before Christ, announce a Messiah who would bring God's salvation to all peoples. When Messiah Jesus finally was on the scene, his ministry was not chiefly at Jerusalem, the center of Judaism, but out in the mixed area: Galilee of the Gentiles. Through his ministry, Jesus made it clear that he had come as Messiah for all peoples who are ready to faithfully follow him. That's the first reason why it is easy, natural and even mandatory for Christians to have a significant cross-cultural worldview.

The second reason is "For here we have no lasting city, but we seek the city that is to come" (Hebrews 13:14). And Paul reminds us that "our citizenship is in heaven, and from it we await a Savior, the Lord Jesus Christ" (Philippians 3:20). In this life, Christians are already cross-cultural creatures. Our passport says Guinea-Bissau or U.S. but our first loyalty and our manner of living say that our primary identity is the unbounded kingdom of heaven.

The Unmaking of an American

Thus, it is an easy, natural thing for Christians to live and to be cross-cultural. It comes with the territory of our faithfulness to Christ and with the maturing of our faith. As a young man, I gave two years of service for Christ in Morocco. When I returned to the USA in 1960, I discovered much of my identity and self-perception as an American, along with my worldview, had undergone profound and irreversible change. I had become a cross-cultured international. During the ensuing forty years of preparation and waiting on the Lord for my return to Africa, I lived a somewhat enigmatic existence of being in, but not of, North American culture.

When I returned to Africa in 2000, it seemed to make sense that I would do a mission term of perhaps seven years and then return to North America and do whatever one does when reaching age 67 and beginning a retirement life. However, about the time I was two-thirds the way through the seven-year term, I could see that my cultural identity was continuing to evolve. There was a push and a pull happening deep inside.

I felt the pull to continue in Africa and stay with the ministry the Lord had opened for me. Africa is where I was needed, where my missional gifts were sought and could continue to be used in the extension of God's kingdom.

In Africa, as one ages, he gains increased value because what he has to say comes out of years of accumulating insights through the experience of life. The elderly are valued and revered as a source of wisdom, steadfastness and perseverance. In contrast, the North American trajectory of aging is the opposite; one's value decreases with age and the movement is towards irrelevancy, dependency and ultimately being humorously ignored. Pondering those two options left me with little doubt where I wanted to be during the remaining years of my life.

Moreover, with the advancement of communication and travel technology, I was still able to remain actively connected to my North American friends, family and the parts of my North American identity I want to preserve.

I also felt the concurrent push to stay away from North America. To thoughtful people around the world, North America is becoming a less and less desirable place to be. North America, through the eyes of the outside observer, appears to be in a serious downward spiral economically, politically, spiritually and almost in any way one wants to view it.

I am particularly troubled by the increasing ease of compromise in the North American church. In Africa, where the church is, by comparison, relatively young, there is movement towards increased faithfulness. I am pulled in the direction of serving where I can be an active participant in the movement towards faithfulness, facilitating believers as they realize God's desire for his people.

All these ponderings have been part of my evolving cultural adaptation and identity. Although living in another culture presents many challenges, with a cross-cultured Christian worldview the journey is a whole lot easier, even fun!

Cross-Cultural Challenges

Cross-cultural challenges are two types: First, there are things that strike us as odd, inconvenient, uncomfortable, quirky, disgusting or annoying. For example, as I noted elsewhere, highway travel is highly risky and generally quite uncomfortable. A vehicle designed to carry a driver plus four passengers comfortably, can be loaded with as many as sixteen people! If you join a transport like that, parts of your extremities are dangling outside, and other parts are unidentifiably entangled with those of your fellow passengers. Since the ride is only four miles, you can willingly put up with the momentary discomfort with a smile.

Or, there is the food. These people would eat fish and rice three times a day if they could get it. For me, a meal of fish and rice once every three years is pushing the limits. From my perspective, peanut butter and jelly sandwiches are gourmet up against fish and rice. But a missionary is taught "in Rome do as the Romans do," so fish and rice it is!

Again, the question of who owns what can be the source of much cross-cultural exasperation. In this communal, tribal society, if you have a shirt, a shovel or

A group of youth in the village of Catel.

a tire pump you are not using at the moment, it means you really don't need it and that you ought to "loan" (code for "give") it to the guy who needs it right now. So I give in and loan Fie my lug wrench if he promises to bring it back no later than 5 p.m. that same day. Two weeks later, the wrench is still not back, and I track down Fie and see if there is any way I can get my lug wrench back. Having recovered it, I am obliged to stay long enough to listen to all the reasons why he failed to keep his agreement.

One day as I was headed out the driveway on my way to a bike ride, a twenty-year-old Christian man, who is active in a nearby church, caught up with me and asked if he could borrow my wheelbarrow. My house was locked but the wheelbarrow was outside so I told him to go get it. When I returned from my bike ride, curiously, there was a pair of well-worn thong sandals on my veranda. I left them there, thinking that the owner would come back to get them.

However, that evening when I was ready to shut down for the day, I hunted in vain to find my house sandals. I was sure I had left them under the veranda bench when I left for the bike ride ten hours earlier. I started putting two and two together so I picked up the worn thongs and took them to the young man's uncle to let him sort out the dilemma.

The next day as I was visiting the uncle, the young nephew showed up. Right away his uncle asked him, "Do you have Forrester's sandals at your house"? When he admitted he did, the uncle ordered him to return them. In a few minutes, I was back in possession of my comfortable, much beloved, house sandals. The young man got a brief but sharp shaming lecture from his uncle. I simply shook hands with him, slapped him on the back and thanked him for returning my sandals.

Challenges of this type are grist for expat bull sessions with each of us trying to outdo the other with incredibly frustrating cross-cultural scenarios.

New-Creation Roadblocks

The second package is made up of cross-cultural challenges that seriously get in the way of the creation of Christian community and are blockages to persons being recreated into the image of Christ. At the Mennonite mission, we are attempting, for example, to address the poverty issue by creating small businesses using local food and fiber resources. Value-added processing of local resources can produce consumer-ready food and clothing items that can be an exit from poverty. With a jump start of initial capital from the outside, we work alongside entrepreneurs to create locally owned and operated small business enterprises.

While we are able to bring together the inputs for creation of such businesses, we have still run into significant cultural challenges and obstacles limiting the success of enterprises that in theory should have created improved living standards. What makes it so difficult to get a small business up and running?

1. Most people are either illiterate or have a literacy level so low that they are unable to do even the most basic bookkeeping or read a business document.

2. Most people are not socially ready to adjust to daily routines and long-term commitment fitting them into a workday model of eight hours of labor dedicated to the operation of the enterprise.

3. A successful, growing enterprise requires one to set aside a portion of the profits for maintenance and expansion. In this culture, however, one is obligated to assist those in desperate fixes by dipping into the reserves. If anyone suspects you have reserves, it is soon common knowledge, and multitudes of your brothers in need will be descending on your door.

There is no way around it: getting out of poverty requires certain skills and the willingness to develop those skills; it also requires a certain level of diligence to participate in the local economy. We continue to struggle to find our way through these obstacles. We believe there is a sure-footed track out of poverty, but getting one's feet on that path is indeed challenging.

Another area with seemingly insurmountable obstacles is the area of family life, specifically marriage. We, along with our African brethren, believe God's model for the family is that one man and one woman will make a lifelong commitment of faithfulness to each other. Although this nuclear family style commitment can happen even in the African context of the strong extended family phenomenon, getting into that pattern has been fraught with cultural challenges.

African Christians continue to place a high value on meeting the traditional social norms of marriage. They are not yet ready to dump all the cultural baggage of seeking extended family affirmation for a union and meeting the dowry expectations of the bride's family. Nor do they need to.

The bride price, however, is so high that in their poverty they are unable to meet dowry expectations. Consequently, we have mostly "shack-up" unofficial marriages, even in the church. With the ever present pressure of hormonal realities, babies come along and the couple live together unable to meet either the expectations of their tradition or the biblical faith model.

In both of the economic and family life areas, significant cultural challenges obstruct transitioning and transformation into the wholeness that comes with following godly principles for life. The transitions happen progressively as people shift from animism into a Christian worldview. While worldview transformation is inherent in the gospel, getting to transformation requires great patience, understanding and grace on the part of those in spiritual leadership, be he an African pastor or an expatriate missionary.

A Patron-Client, Honor-Shame Culture

Probably no cultural characteristic causes the expatriate missioner more vexation than these quintessential bedrock features of West African culture. Number one on the African's psycho-social need is finding one's place in the social scale and maintaining one's niche through good, proper, and right relationships. Although North Americans also would like good relationships, that goal is trumped by the need to be independent and successful. Our societies operate with vastly different priorities.

In Africa, right relationships are maintained through careful observation of the unwritten codes of patron-client interaction. For those above you on the social scale, you have the role of client or vassal; for those below you, you are their patron. Right relationships are maintained as honor, homage and loyalty flow upward from client to patron and, in return, protection, assistance and favors flow down from patron to client. Failure in relationships brings shame when the patron lacks benevolence or the client messes up in offering homage to the patron.

North Americans coming from the powerful, wealthy West are automatically viewed as desirable patron candidates. Immediately upon arrival in West Africa, newcomers are plied by Africans who are only doing what their mothers taught them to do: find patrons. They groom us as potential patrons with proffered homage and offers of ingratiating hospitality that are thinly veiled attempts at establishing client-patron liaisons. We find it very difficult to handle social patterns the Africans view as completely normal, desirable and acceptable. We are egalitarians, eschewing begging or patronizing; we squirm embarrassingly under such a social order, not sure what to do with it.

For Mennonite missionaries, who place a high value on servanthood, to be the object of someone's homage, allegiance, praise and flattery is cause for wincing. Our open hearts and hands are exactly what the patron-seeking African is looking for. It takes some years of experience before the Westerner becomes able to navigate adroitly and courteously the social waters of West Africa and come through the patron-client ordeal unscathed and not ready to pack up and leave. It is very wearing on Westerners to have people constantly badgering us to become their patron. We feel trivialized by people wanting to be our friend solely for the sake of what they can get out of us.

Mennonite missionaries and visitors generally arrive in West Africa in Dakar, Senegal. We stay at a missionary guesthouse before continuing on our way another four hundred miles south to MCWA territory in Gambia and Guinea-Bissau. Patrice, a care-taker at the guesthouse, is like a ten-year-old with the enviable task of clerking at a candy store. Although, he is honestly friendly and welcoming, all the while he maintains his other agenda of finding patrons among visitors at the guesthouse.

Patrice has helped me immensely in dealing with the lech-erous baggage handlers and taxi hustlers at the Dakar airport. I couldn't do my visitor logistics in Dakar without his assistance. As expected, however, he comes, on cue, with a request for my patronage with his daughter's school fees.

Before moving to Guinea-Bissau, while I was still in Pirang, Gambia, I acquired an eleven-passenger van for the mission. We owned it for about seven years, and while it was indispensible for our outreach and general mission logistics, the van was a never-ending source of agony in the push and pull of client-patron obligations. Because I was welcomed and honored by the villagers, they had earned rights to free taxi service in the van, especially when needing transport in relation to a funeral, the ultimate in social obligations.

One time in Pirang, some of the villagers asked for transportation to a funeral in a village about eight miles up the road. I agreed to take them but with two conditions: One, I would not carry more than fourteen passengers in my van (they would have packed in twenty), and two, I needed to return to Pirang by 6:00 p.m. for another meeting. (Funerals go on for days). The passengers agreed to both stipulations. Nevertheless, when the time came to leave for the funeral, I got shamed for not taking along the additional six people who wanted to get in the van. And later in the evening, I was shamed for leaving for my 6:00 p.m. appointment before my passengers were ready to depart from a half-finished funeral. This tale of Forrester's rudeness traveled all the way back to the mission headquarters in Pennsylvania.

In Catel, the villagers welcomed us cordially and graciously as a site to locate our mission in Guinea-Bissau. But driving the welcome were very high expectations for our patronage: that somehow our benevolence would lavish on them a prosperous, easy, carefree, materialistic life. We didn't promise them anything of the sort, but our conversation registered in their minds as a promise, driven by the social codes of the patron-client relationship.

When their dreams of magical prosperity were not realized, shaming us kicked in as the way to deal with their unfulfilled expectations of us who had been elevated to patrons. In time a pre-school, clinic, and other community amenities were established, but only as the villagers joined us in the process of community transformation. That process is ongoing.

The expatriate missionary needs to be very careful during simple, friendly conversation with the Africans, since merely showing an interest in what they are doing is read as a promise for patronizing intervention. For example, if I bump into Mario and ask him how it's going with his house building project, my interest signals an opportunity for him to implore my patronage. The conversation quickly moves from a casual friendly inquiry to, "Can you loan (give) me money for the roof corrugate because soon the rains will come and my walls will be ruined. All my work on the house will be lost." He will even go so far as to remind me that Jesus taught us to help those with this sort of need.

What does a missionary do? It's a conundrum I still haven't totally resolved. We are here among these impoverished, margin-alized people because of their enormous physical needs, and we are here because our Teacher instructed us to materially share with those in need. Our assistance, however, can have the long-term effect of entrenching their poverty and dependency on handouts and never really enabling them to escape poverty. The easy reso-lution is simply not to be in Africa or anyplace where we bump into Marios. We can stay within the gated West and philosophize about those on the outside. But if we do that, we still need to deal with the example and teaching of the One we worship as Lord.

Yet another non-solution was offered in a conversation I once had with an Australian missionary. He self-righteously reminded me that in their mission they "don't do projects, just preach the gospel." Okay.

When Jesus was in our situation, he also was tempted to take the shortcut and make sacrifice go away, take the easy route out: make bread out of stones, parachute into the temple courtyard and be given authority by a trickster. His resolution

YESer's Andrew Stutzman and Peter Stahl with some of their friends.

was to stay the course of suffering and sacrifice alongside those he came to transform, and the results have been Edenic and out of this world: the establishment of God's new community transformed by both unbounded love and solid faithfulness to the Father's designs. The missional community is fueled by the same commitment.

In this quest I have been helped by turning my vision on the potential and the promise of the new creation in the lives of individuals and communities. For example, in Catel one of my dear friends is Momadu. He has an unforgettable face. It is marred by a crisscross of scars, a grim reminder of the day he and his dad duked it out with machetes. His dad was a cattle rustler, making his living by crossing into Senegal to round up livestock. When cattle rustlers are doing their thing in Senegal, soldiers have orders to shoot them on sight, no questions asked. The soldiers' ploy is to shoot one of the men, watch for someone to come soon to retrieve the body of his comrade, then shoot him as well. The bodies are left for the vultures. That's how Momadu's dad met his end.

A similar fate awaits Momadu unless he is transformed by Jesus. I cannot give up hope for him even though he drinks heavily, is frequently in fights, spends time in prison and goes through life in deep darkness. He has told us he wants to change and has even attended church occasionally. But so far, not much has happened. Still, we don't give up hope. I imagine him someday to be a great man of God, who, because of what he has been through, is able to minister to those who are prisoners of Satan and living life on the bottom.

I have other African friends who, in their conduct and attitudes, are outstanding models of kindness, joy, and justice, as well as leaders in their communities. They are already models of everything a Christian should be, so close, but till now unwilling to come under the Lordship of Jesus and join the community of faith. Still, we don't give up hope.

Having this kind of passion and vision for individuals help to override the unanswered, puzzling ambiguities of cross-cultural mission.

There are very few people left who have their heads so deep in the sand that they still think that it is the special burden of the church in the North to be carrying the Gospel to the people in the South. It is no longer news that the center of paganism, secularism and atheism has moved up the globe and now dominates the North. The South has a growing spiritual hunger, and in most seekers' minds Jesus Christ is at the center of their quest.

But Christians in the South are generally not equipped theologically, technologically and financially to take on the North as an evangelistic challenge. Southerners lack the sophistication and adroitness to witness to the North. But perhaps the day will come when in a mighty way God will again make foolish the wisdom of the wise and the called will confess Christ the power of God and the wisdom of God. For the foolishness of God is wiser than men, and the weakness of God is stronger than men (see 1 Corinthians 1:20-25).

In the early years of the First Century church, it soon became evident that the church would be multicultural, drawing believers from all ethnic backgrounds. The early leaders were willing to accept people from other cultures provided the others were willing to give up their culture and become Jews, much like missionaries from a bygone era assumed that African believers needed to be westernized. But that isn't God's plan. When people become Christian they bring their culture with them and the entire church is enriched by the learning that happens when the church is multiethnic.

Listen to the Apostle Peter's amazement as he and his fellow leaders made that discovery: "As I began to speak, the Holy Spirit fell on them just as on us at the beginning. And I remembered the word of the Lord, how he said, 'John baptized with water, but you will be baptized with the Holy Spirit.' If then God gave the same gift to them as he gave to us when we believed in the Lord Jesus Christ, who was I that I could stand in God's way?" When they heard these things they fell silent. And they glorified God, saying, "Then to the Gentiles also God has granted repentance that leads to life" (Acts 11: 15-18).

In Romans 2 Paul takes it a step further. In his argument that Jews have no advantage over the Gentiles in relation to God just because they are God's chosen people, Paul tells his Jewish readers that the Gentiles, even before becoming Christian, have various aspects of God's law written on their conscience and are able to make moral decisions based on this inherent human quality endowed to all mankind by our Creator. Thus Paul says the Gentiles are just as able to live godly as much as a Jew who has the Torah.

One of the fascinating discoveries awaiting the cross cultural missionary in Africa is to uncover ways the Africans already live (or had lived before they were Westernized) by God's moral law, even prior to the arrival of the Christian missionary. Let me mention some culturally practiced godly principles I have found among my African friends, both Christian and non-Christian. These vary according to ethnic group:

- Obey and honor your elders.

- Welcome and be hospitable to the stranger.

- Sexual relations are only for a man and a woman who are married to each other. (This moral belief declined during the sexual revolution wave that swept across Africa from Europe and America in the 1960s.)

- Sexual relations between persons of the same gender are not allowed.

- Do not steal, respect the personal property of others especially to those of your ethnic group (this moral also has disappeared).

- Economic and material equality is preferred over inequality; your abundance must be shared with the community

- The community's well-being and will have precedence over that of the individual

No doubt there are others I have yet to learn about. But this is enough to tell us how much the church in the West could learn by listening and being taught by our African brothers and sisters from their culturally inherent godliness.

A Cultural Challenge Story

It was a chilly January night with the temperature in the mid sixties. That's downright frigid when your body is accustomed to the ambience of the mid nineties. Because I didn't have a blanket or enough clothing to stay warm, I had a problem getting comfortable on the cement slab where I was attempting to get some sleep after a twelve-hour bone-jarring bush-taxi ride. My trip from Dakar to my home in southern Senegal, had come to a temporary halt in the village of Kandlediou, Senegal, about a hundred miles away from my destination.

Tossing and turning on that cold cement slab of a tumbledown store front in nowhere Kandlediou, I was having a conversation with God interspersed with my mind's recording of a hymn line I had been singing for the past seventy years: "Must I be carried to the skies on flowery beds of ease?" Evidently not. Still, as I gazed up at the stars billions of miles away, I wanted to make sense of why I, a 73-year-old missionary, now found myself in this uncomfortable situation. I wasn't angry or complaining; I just wanted to know why. In my previous sixteen years as a missionary in Africa, I had been through dozens of trying, unsavory situations; however, at 73 and now fictionally retired, I somehow thought I wasn't supposed to be doing those anymore. Apparently I still hadn't arrived at missionary nirvana.

I had needed to spend an entire week in Dakar in order to get visas for Sierra Leone and Ghana where I would be spending two months in a teaching, consulting role with other African missions. I was prepared to spend two weeks just getting the visas into my passport, but miraculously the Ghana embassy had reduced the time for granting visas from five to a mere three days. On Wednesday with that one in place, I dashed off to the Sierra Leone embassy and discovered it took them only 24 hours to paste in the visa. All this made it possible to catch the Friday, overnight ferry back to Ziguinchor. What a coup!

Except that I was suddenly made aware that the previous ferry trip had been cancelled because of high seas, and my Friday ferry was fully booked for the passengers who had not succeeded on the Wednesday trip. I, along with all 400 other Friday passengers, got bumped to the following week.

Since I had no desire to spend several more days in the teaming Dakar metropolis, I took my only other option: go the torturous 400 miles by bush taxi. It had been five years since I endured that punishment and vowed never to put myself through that trauma again. However, the only way to avert another week in Dakar was to run the bush taxi gauntlet.

Patrice, my friend at the guesthouse, helped me get a taxi for the five mile ride across town to the Gare Routière (bus station).

As we were cutting across town, the taxi driver kept leaning out the window looking down at the front left tire. We needed to stop three times during the ride to get it pumped. Finally, at the last stop the driver declared the tire flat and he could go no farther. He refunded a dollar of the fare and I was on my own to go by foot the final quarter mile. I had my backpack full of the week's necessities including my minibook. Also I had two buckets of ornamental nursery stock for the plant nursery I was starting in Ziguinchor. I was struggling under the weight but made it with the help of a gentleman who went part of the way with me just to make sure I stayed on track to the station.

At the station, I boarded a seven-passenger Peugeot designed to comfortably carry five. The back bench is perched above the rear axle, and it is fine if you happen to have the spinal column of a five-footer. Rather than ride in back, I waited for the next taxi to get a front or middle seat.

Finally at 3:00 p.m., we were on our way south out of Dakar and heading for the Gambia border and a ferry crossing of the Gambia River. Africa's smallest country, Gambia, is essentially the river banks of the River Gambia. Roughly fifteen miles wide and 150 miles long, it is an enigmatic piece of geography that had no reason to become a country but was a leftover from the colonial days.

We arrived in total darkness at the border just a few minutes before the nine p.m. closing time. At the Sénégal exit immigration, a voice rang out, Forresta, que' est ce que tu fais ici? ("What are you doing here?") He was an officer previously stationed at Mpak where I crossed frequently from Guinea-Bissau. He quickly stamped my passport and I hurried off to the riverside Gambia immigration to get a transit visa for the passage across Gambia. Getting there involved another four-mile taxi ride in a dilapidated Peugeot with only parking lights for lighting the road ahead. With the roughness of the road, the headlights finally, mercifully connected. At the Gambia immigration office, one of the officers kindly helped me carry my plant buckets down to the ferry just as it was landing for its last trip back across the river. Had we been ten minutes later, I would have spent the night at the riverside.

The six of us going to Ziguinchor stayed together because it was easier to get a taxi with that many people. After re-entering Senegal, we got a taxi to Ziguinchor, and I thought we might arrive there about daybreak the next morning, but that wasn't to be.

About ten miles down the road, the Senegal military had a road block, and no traffic was allowed to continue to Ziguinchor until daylight the next morning because of the risk of attack by highway bandits. In the daylight, plenty of traffic and soldiers are on patrol, keeping the bandits in the bush. At night, they rule the highway, and no prudent driver ventures past the Kandlediou military post. That's where and why I ended up on the cement slab.

Sheer fatigue finally set in and I must have dozed off for at least a few minutes because I had a dream. Most of my dreams have a common template: I find myself in a remote, primitive area dealing with one sort or another of an impossible quandary that resolves itself only by my waking up. This dream was a replay of that familiar script.

I finally gave up on the idea of sleep and joined a campfire of other travelers stalled in Kandlediou for the night. Most of them were youth on their way north to a Muslim festival in northern Senegal. Although I wanted to join them in the conversation, our interchange was very limited because they had gone through Arabic school and spoke little French, and I spoke no Wolof.

"Weary was our heart with waiting and the night-watch seemed so long; but his triumph-day is breaking, and we hail it with a song!" (another one of my hymn tracks). At 7:00 a.m. the old tire roadblock was lifted, and we made fast tracks toward Ziguinchor.

Finally, at 10:00 a.m., I was back at my sweet oval cottage in Bourofaye, not much the worse for the wear, and with another story to share, because the gospel we bring is cross-cultural.

Chapter 7

Forming the Community of Christ in the West African Animistic Context

The community of Christ is a living organism in every sense. It is the bride, the spouse of Christ, the living Lord of the church. The community is made up of flesh and blood people adopted into the family of God. The community becomes a reflection of the Eternal One for whom and by whom it has been called into existence. Wherever the community of Christ is found in the world, regardless of culture, it will reflect persons who have been recreated into the divine image of our Creator God. This new community becomes the very stage upon which the entire world and cosmos watch the unfolding of God's "plan for the fullness of time, to unite all things in him [Christ], things in heaven and things on earth" (Ephesians 1:10).

Two scriptures are essential in our understanding of what it means to become a community of Christ:

"As you come to him, a living stone rejected by men but in the sight of God chosen and precious, you yourselves like living stones are being built up as a spiritual house, to be a holy priesthood, to offer spiritual sacrifices acceptable to God through Jesus Christ" (1Peter 2: 4-5).

"Blessed be the God and Father of our Lord Jesus Christ, who has blessed us in Christ with every spiritual blessing in the heavenly places, even as he chose us in him before the foundation of the world, that we should be holy and blameless before him. In love he predestined us for adoption as sons through Jesus Christ, according to the purpose of his will, to the praise of his glorious grace, with which he has blessed us in the Beloved. In him we have redemption through his blood, the forgiveness of our trespasses, according to the riches of his grace, which he lavished upon us, in all wisdom and insight making known to us the mystery of his will, according to his purpose, which he set forth in Christ as a plan for the fullness of time, to unite all things in him, things in heaven and things on earth" (Ephesians 1: 8-10).

Here we highlight some of the faith and community qualities that become evident as the believers grow into faithful disciples of Jesus and transition from animism into a community of Christ. These qualities are identity tags that one picks up and takes along on the journey. They are the autographs of an emergent people on their way into Christ.

We are an Exodus people

When I began teaching the Bible to the seekers in Catel in 2005, I quickly saw how they were attracted to Bible stories— especially stories from the life of Jesus, how he interacted with people just like themselves, addressing the same challenges they face. One of the joys of teaching the Bible here comes from the fact that this culture shares so much in common with the culture and worldview of biblical times. These people find it far easier than a North American audience to relate to the biblical context.

These are a visual/oral/story-oriented people. Communicating and teaching about God happens most effectively when telling a story of God's interaction if I have a pictorial representation to authenticate the story. In this culture, illustrations have a higher value than they do for a Western audience. The audience becomes glued to the poster-size illustrations. Watching their eyes and faces as they listen, I realize that from their perspective, what they see on the drawing is not just the artist's abstract idea of what happened; it is the equivalent to a photographic representation of what actually happened.

I picked up on another point the Lord was telling me about communicating and teaching the folks in Catel: the Bible stories needed to portray African images and people. Otherwise they were seeing the Christian faith as a white man's religion. And why not? The people on the white missionary's posters are white folks.

I became aware of this need as we showed the Jesus video most Sunday evenings at the Catel meetinghouse. In this two-hour video on the life of Christ, there is exactly one black man among the throngs around Jesus. He shows up for one whole second as the mob is following Jesus through the streets of Jerusalem to Golgotha. There he is, a full-blown black guy, just like themselves! As the camera pans across the crowd and his face comes into view, I detect a murmuring approval move across the spectators there in the meetinghouse. That lit the fire I needed to put me in pursuit of Bible pictures that portray Africans. This was 2008.

In my teaching, I was focusing mostly on the life of Christ because, in my own spirit, I sensed the people's need to hear about a Man who came from God to live among them conveying God's love, forgiveness, hope, deliverance, and a new life—the Messiah.

But I could not just tell the story of Jesus without at least occasionally picking up on the events of the millennia prior to the Advent. One of the Old Testament stories with obvious appeal and application is the Exodus account. As I studied the Exodus event, I became more and more fascinated with how the historic Exodus is the story of God's victory over the demonic powers of Guinea-Bissau. Setting Bissauans free to worship God and become his people takes nothing less than a spiritual and cosmic Exodus.

The Islamic and most of the Christian faith communities already present in Guinea-Bissau wanted to have it both ways: Give lip service to the Lord God and at the same time rely on the satanic forces as their primary source for spiritual power.

In the Mennonite community, we would settle for nothing less than total freedom from the evil Pharaonic powers dominating this land. We stand with the Almighty who said, "Let my people go that they may serve me." No one was prepared to emigrate; we stake our claim right here in Guinea-Bissau, claiming it for the kingdom of God. In this community of Messiah Jesus, we are free to serve (worship) the Creator God and live in his holiness.

Being set free from the powers of evil became a hallmark of the Bissau Mennonite community of believers. To illustrate the Exodus story, I needed an Africanized pictorial of it. To make that happen I connected with the Mennonite artist, Liz Hess, in Lancaster, Pennsylvania. My synapse with Liz came via an epiphany and the help of Kaylene Derksen at EMM.

I communicated with Liz the need for an Africanized visual of the Exodus story specifically tailored to the spiritual realities of Guinea-Bissau. I needed a tableau portraying God's people being liberated from the awfulness of satanic slavery, their travels through the wilderness and the arrival in the Promised Land.

In 2009 the finished three-panel painting was delivered to us in Catel by Lancaster Christian radio host, Lisa Landis. As soon as I saw the finished work, I knew the church in Guinea-Bissau had been gifted with a major teaching tool. I was in awe at the way Liz had used her artistic gifts to communicate what has to be the watershed salvation motif of history: God's defeat of Satan as he delivers his covenant people from Egypt into the land promised to Abraham. These three canvases express God's salvation message in a way that can easily be understood by a typical animistic Bissauan.

The first of the 18x24-inch panels is dominated by a muscular dark-skinned Satan, silhouetted against the fires of hell. He is a stylized figure complete with short horns, pointed ears,

 and glowing elliptical eyes and a flying whip in his right hand. The background says "Egypt" with its pyramids surrounding Satan. In front of him and under the whip are several, obviously African,

men and women, manacled and in slave garb, totally without hope and dominated by the satanic taskmaster.

The second panel continues the Egypt setting for its first four inches, but then there is the departure from Egypt delineated by the cross. As the African figures pass the cross, their shackles fly off, and they are in the wilderness, a vast, lifeless landscape, but a free people on their way to the Promised Land.

In the sky above the distant mountains, is a faintly discernible image of the face of Christ, with his outstretched hand full of pure white light: his invitation to come and follow his way through the trackless wilderness. Here the narrator explains that the wilderness trek is a learning experience for those set free by the defeat of the taskmaster, accomplished by the sacrifice of Christ on the cross. On the way to the Promised Land, we learn what it means to reclaim our heritage as God's chosen people. We learn to trust God for all our needs, confident that he will fight the battles for us as he forms us into a special redeemed people destined to showcase his glory to all of creation. We acknowledge that on the trek to the Promised Land, there are struggles, doubts and even times of rebellion and the temptation to relapse to Egypt. However, the wilderness is a not-to-be-missed discipling stage on the way to becoming God's people.

The third panel portrays the arrival in the Promised Land as the pilgrims leap from behind a gushing waterfall into a verdant, colorful paradise-landscape of flowing water, fruit trees and happy people. Here the central feature is the outstretched, welcoming, but nail-pierced hands of the Savior. They are the hands of a black King of Kings and Lord of Lords. Everyone rushes to his embrace.

The narrator explains that the benefits of the Promised Land are something we already enjoy now as we live day by day in the care and nurture of our Shepherd Jesus within the Christian faith community. But in the future those blessings will be experienced in a fulfillment we can now scarcely imagine.

The creator of the three panels, artist Liz Hess, comments on the spiritual experience of illustrating the Exodus story in the Guinea-Bissau context:

This painting was much bigger than me or my artistic gifts. I went forward praying the Holy Spirit would equip me specifically for the task, much like he equipped the artisans of old for the particular call to design the wilderness tabernacle. When I sat down to begin the project, the inspiration hit me with a bang and would not shut off.

That first day of work, when I put down my brush for the night and attempted to get some sleep, I just lay there, wide awake seeing various details in my mind that needed to be incorporated on the canvases. Finally, I gave up on sleeping and went back into the studio and continued to paint until four in the morning.

The second night into the project, again just as I was drifting off to sleep, I saw an image of the face of Christ that needed to go into the middle panel. I managed to store that in my memory, and the next day my hands and mind worked furiously putting onto the canvas the vision I had the evening before.

What I had anticipated would be a significant challenge turned into being a labor of sheer joy, excitement and ministry deep inside myself. Creating the last panel, the arrival in the Promised Land was a genuine time of worship for me as I felt what the characters on the canvas must be feeling as at last, after the arduous journey, they come upon the cool waters of refreshment in a garden of rest, and there in the midst of paradise are the welcoming arms of Jesus. Nothing of the difficulties along the route to the Promised Land will compare to the joy one day of seeing him face to face.

It is with deep humility and great honor that I have been chosen for this task. To feel the inspiration of the Holy Spirit through my brushes was an experience I would love to have every time I paint. I wish I could feel that same ease, flow and momentum that accompanied this project. From the very first brush stroke till the last, these three canvases were created in just two and a half days not because I rushed or was in a hurry, but because the images flowed out and I could not shut them off even when I attempted to get some sleep.

I have finished my task with this painting, but the journey of the work is just beginning. As the artist, I ask God to anoint them to accomplish the ministry he has designed for them.

At the front of our meetinghouse in Catel, we have a framed copy of the three Exodus panels. I asked some of the church leaders what the paintings mean to them. One replied, "Those paintings are the story of my life. I was once totally enslaved to Satan. The first panel accurately conveys the terrible life in Satan's kingdom. He controlled everything I did. I lived in constant fear and obligation to Satan's power. But when the missionaries came and began to teach us God's Word, I began to see that there was a far better way to live, that was through faith and obedience to Christ. Now I am on the journey to the Promised Land and I make that journey in the light of Christ. I am reminded of that every time I come to church and see those paintings."

Another leader explained, "When I see that first panel, it reminds me of how Satan had me enslaved in an existence—the alcoholism, the anger, the evil for evil—all that is a life I never, never want to experience again. And even though the journey through the wilderness is not always easy, I know that I have been received by Jesus and I persevere because I am assured that one day, when this life is over, I will be received into his eternal kingdom of peace, joy and plenty."

A New Identity as God's People

"But you are a chosen race, a royal priesthood, a holy nation, a people for his own possession, that you may proclaim the excellencies of him who called you out of darkness into his marvelous light. Once you were not a people, but now you are God's people; once you had not received mercy, but now you have received mercy. . . To this end we always pray for you, that our God may make you worthy of his calling and may fulfill every resolve for good and every work of faith by his power, so that the name of our Lord Jesus may be glorified in you, and you in him, according to the grace of our God and the Lord Jesus Christ" (1 Peter 2:9-12).

These verses from 1 Peter 2 speak about people coming into a new identity, about an old story merging into a new story and about adopting a new center for life. These are all foundational changes that happen to a people group that moves from not being God's people to becoming part of his worldwide family.

The pioneer missionary is present for this change of identity. He is a facilitator, a sort of mid-wife for the event. The transition can happen only by the power and the work of the Holy Spirit, but it is attended and helped along by the pioneer missionary, who needs to be strong of heart, spirit, mind and body.

It's about helping people find their way from being "not a people" to becoming God's people and from being outsiders to joining the family that lives by the mercy and grace of God, made worthy of his calling and fulfilling in them every resolve for good and every work of faith in their lives as a faith community. It has been my joy to witness the merging of these "no people" into the story of God's family.

I will never forget the despair and sadness I saw on my first exposure to the Balanta community in the village of Pirang, Gambia, a few days before Christmas 2002. I was taken to their enclave by my Muslim friend, Sulayman, after he had asked me if I would like to meet some Christians in Pirang, the village where I eventually took up residence and built a mission center six miles east of Brikama, Gambia.

The Balantas had migrated to Gambia from Guinea-Bissau because of the war and poverty in Guinea-Bissau. Although they were not welcomed in Gambia, they came and stayed anyway. Illegal immigrants without status or protection, they could not be hired as legal workers and were forced to survive on agriculture and fishing or as abused clandestine laborers. Considered "dogs" because they refused to convert to Islam, they could not get medical care, and their children could not attend public schools. They were among the region's most marginalized people. Or, to borrow the phrase from 1 Peter 2, they "were not a people." Their identity was nothing anyone wanted to acknowledge or even talk about.

Even in their Guinea-Bissau homeland where they are the majority ethnic group, the Balantas are regarded by other ethnic groups as on the lowest rung of society. They are least educated, the most backward, the most warlike, and the first to use physical violence, the least trusted, the most into demonic practices and on and on.

Try to imagine what it would be like to go from that identity, transitioning into God's chosen, holy people and heirs of God's kingdom!

I can never erase from my memory the scene of their compound on the outskirts of Pirang. A tumbledown mud brick hut unfit for habitation housed 25 to 30 people. In the back, the men gathered, most of them drunk and asleep. The women cooked rice, and a passel of children, many with scabies and impetigo, played in the dirt and filth. It was a snapshot of squalor, hopelessness, and what it is like to be "not a people."

The group leader, Augustine, and probably the only sober man there, welcomed me and found a stool for me to sit with them. After some introductions and get-acquainted exchanges, he looked me in the eyes and said, "Forrester, could you come and teach us the Bible?" Without hesitation, I said, "Sure, can we get started this coming Sunday morning?" And so it was, the first steps of a no-people merging into and becoming part of the story of God's people. That was Christmas 2002.

What encourages people to take their first faltering steps towards faith in Christ and begin the trek that enables them to merge their story with God's story? This is a question I have often pondered. I believe the Holy Spirit can use practically any circumstance or happenstance to prod a person towards faith in Christ.

One of the leaders in our church said he attended a church service where the beautiful and spirited singing of the congregation pushed him towards looking more seriously at the truth of Messiah Jesus.

Another said his eyes were opened to the awfulness of life under animism, and he knew there had to be something better than living in constant fear of curses and the obligation of fighting evil with evil.

For some it has been a physical healing or deliverance from evil dreams. For others it is just the presence of the missionary. One day I went to a village to conduct a service, as we did weekly. I was met at the compound gate by a young woman with sparkling eyes and a mile-wide smile on her face. She said, "I know the message of God you are sharing with us is the truth because no one would have left his home and travelled halfway around the world to tell us this if it wasn't the truth!"

For the people at the Balanta compound in Pirang, I believe it was the wretchedness of their living conditions, the sickness and the hopelessness dominating their lives that propelled at least some of them to reason that, if there is a God, surely there must be something better than this.

These are the seeds of faith that, if nurtured and treasured, can eventually bloom into one deciding to join his or her story to the story of God's people and claim the heritage of being part of God's family.

But what does it mean to merge with God's chosen people? The apostle Paul speaks of adoption into God's family. "For you did not receive the spirit of slavery to fall back into fear, but you have received the Spirit of adoption as sons, by whom we cry, 'Abba! Father!'" (Romans 8:15). According to this verse we have received the Spirit of adoption, meaning that the Holy Spirit has transferred us into God's family. That is to say, in terms of righteousness, the Spirit qualifies us through his power to be God's children. The covenants and promises God made to Abraham are now ours. The Spirit enables us to live in the manner that brings glory to our Father God.

Jesus spoke of this relationship as abiding, we in God and God in us (John 14). There are exactly two indicators of the mutual abiding: obedience to his commands and love. Heirs in God's family begin to look and act like our elder brother, Jesus, defining one's new identity in God's family, a transition I have witnessed in West Africa.

We believe that God is already active and present in all cultures. Why abandon one's culture and adopt a "Christian culture" from another part of the world? The Mennonite mission has no expectations of doing that. We believe the Holy Spirit enables us to discern the good things of God in our cultures, but those aspects of culture that are outside his design for his people, he enables us to transform.

Why is the issue of identity so important for believers in West Africa? It is because here we have an honor-shame society. Life is about finding honor for oneself and using shame to dominate and control others. Being in a position to dominate and manipulate others somehow cumulates to one's personal stash of honor. This system is abetted by satanic power of lies and condemnation. Shame and dishonor are a satanic stronghold he uses to keep people from the dignity and righteousness accorded to us as we are recreated in the image of Jesus.

With our adoption as sons of God, comes the worth and dignity of living rightly God's righteousness. As sons and daughters accepted by God, we need nothing more to authenticate our value and status. We are freed from needing to be either a doormat or a bullying intimidator. We all stand together in the equality of brothers and sisters of Christ. The identity we receive in God's family lifts the downtrodden and humbles the mighty.

The Community of Christ: Servanthood

"You know that the rulers of the Gentiles lord it over them, and their great ones exercise authority over them. It shall not be so among you. But whoever would be great among you must be your servant, and whoever would be first among you must be your slave, even as the Son of Man came not to be served but to serve, and to give his life as a ransom for many" (Matthew 20:25-28). Also, "But I am among you as the one who serves" (Luke 22:27).

The pioneer mission team in Gambia and Guinea-Bissau made it a goal to model a community of servanthood in day to day ministry activities:

- Having a level of compassion that gets us close enough to people to hear and see their stories, their hurts, their needs and hopes

- Embodying God's love, grace, and transforming power in our own lives

- Teaching the story of God's saving, transforming, and rec-reating intervention with mankind and all of his creation as recorded in the Bible

- Being involved with and assisting people to find solutions to their needs, particularly by using resources God has already placed in their communities

- Helping people to take responsibility for ways they have violated God's will and encouraging them to connect with God's transforming power

- Connecting the community with outside resources in ways that foster local innovation and ownership

- Taking the lead in the formation of a faith community of those seeking to follow Jesus

This is the vision and the task of servanthood that I commend to everyone contemplating affiliation with the Mennonite Church

West Africa (MCWA) faith community, expatriate missionaries or African church leaders.

Understanding that Jesus came as a servant rather than a master is a key factor of our Christology and points us in the direction of Anabaptist ecclesiology. Everything about God's agenda for the ages and his plan to redeem his creation happens in the context of loving, freely-offered and sacrificial servanthood, giving one's life for the sake of bringing God's salvation to others. Without the laying down of one's life, there is no resurrection to new life. Evil is defeated and re-creation is possible; new life comes via life-giving, loving servanthood.

Every year the Mennonites from Gambia, Casamance (southern Senegal) and Guinea Bissau gather for a fellowship conference in Gambia. This group is using a public transport vehicle.

Likewise, what the church today does in terms of mission and proclamation of the Gospel in word and deed can happen only in the context of loving, freely-offered servanthood towards those we are inviting to join God's family. All the gifts God gives us to carry out our ministry (preaching, teaching, healing, prophesying, encouraging), all must be carried out with the heart, the hands and the lips of the humblest of self-sacrificing servants. On the other hand, one desiring to be a master would best become a politician or business person.

In West Africa, it is abnormal for one to be a servant (slave, to use the proper New Testament term). Slave/servant equals shame. No one in his right mind could possibly seek to find fulfillment in a role considered to be shameful. In the past, and even today in Africa, slavery means servitude, low self-esteem, a person of no value, a client who renders total obedience to an honored patron.

This culture lacks anything resembling the Jesus model of greatness coming via slavery, self-sacrifice and servanthood. But that is exactly the lifestyle I believe the Lord requires of his community. Therefore, if the model is absent, it must be modeled by the messengers, the missionaries, just as it was in Christianity's first century by Christ and his apostles in their Palestinian context, also a patron-client culture.

In contrast to the idea of servanthood, a position in the church has great appeal to Africans mainly because it's an opportunity for honor, authority and status above one's fellows. Consequently, church hierarchy is important in African Christian communities. Among some, the hierarchical, "I'm in charge here," authoritarian model is held up to young men as an assured route to fleshly power, wealth, success and comfort. And it's all legitimated by a cherry-picking selection of verses from the Epistles and generous helpings of flat-Bible hermeneutics.

In areas of Africa where the "High Church" has been established for many generations, it is common to find church leaders with titles like, "His Reverence, the Right Doctor Such and Such." Anyone addressing this man is expected to say, "Your Lordship, blah, blah, blah." Under him there will be a multi-rung ladder of other worthies, each with his fetching title of honor.

One particular evangelist bedazzles impoverished young African men with visions of greatness, wealth, honor and power, not to mention the lovely wife, a nice car and a large home. All this is theirs by becoming lead pastors of American-style mega churches they are to create on the African landscape. He equips them to accomplish this by providing four years of highly regimented Bible college where they are students 24/7, dressed in black three-piece suits.

In the Believer's Church context, such pomp and circumstance are out of place. Here we are all just servants and go by our first names or the familial "brother/sister." Anything more than that violates the Lord's requirement for servants. Obviously, there must be roles and positions of leadership and responsibility in the church, but we are all on the same level of worth, just servants of Christ, ministering his love and grace wherever we are. All worth and honor belong to our Father who claims us as sons and daughters. We do not use spiritual gifts or positions in the community of faith to leverage our own personal worth, honor, wealth, authority and esteem.

The fruit of authoritarian kingdom building in the African church is legalism, anemic spirituality, the stifling of spiritual gifts and the lack of assurance of salvation. It even facilitates syncretism. Seeing all of this first hand is the primary reason why I realized the need for a faith community patterned on the Anabaptist, believer's church, living in obedience to the command and example of Christ on this particular issue. Not only is it modeled by the leaders, but it is also expected as normal for all Jesus' followers.

So how did the pioneer mission team in West Africa model Anabaptist Christology and ecclesiology? The short answer is that we became servants of the people to whom we were sent. For starters, we lived among those to whom we came to share the gospel. Some missionaries reside in the city where they have access to most of the comforts and conveniences of Western culture. From the city they go out, campaign-style, into the hinterlands on evangelistic forays.

One day as I was going about work in Catel, I was hearing someone preaching the Gospel on a sound amplification system. It was so clear I thought it was right there in our neighborhood. But on further checking I found that it was coming from Campada, a village a mile away!

An industrial strength version of this model of evangelism occurred in the nearby city of Ziguinchor, Senegal in November 2012.

One day when I was making the oft-repeated border crossing from Guinea-Bissau into Senegal, I met with a cortege of eighteen heavy vehicles, including buses, tractor trailers and beefy 4x4s, waiting to cross into Guinea-Bissau. The vehicles were painted in gaudy colors, and the tag line, "Jesus the Healer," was emblazoned boldly on each. Then I remembered, oh yes, this is the day the evangelistic crusade was pulling out of Ziguinchor and heading back to their home turf in Ghana.

For weeks, prior to their arrival, the town had literally been plastered with billboards and banners advertising the healing campaign about to take place. Each included the tag line and a photo of the mustachioed evangelist. Many churches came together, doing months of preparation in advance of the campaign. Although the campaign budget was undisclosed, it most certainly exceeded $100,000, more than the combined annual budgets for the supporting churches.

The event was held in a large open-air sports stadium with a service each evening beginning at six and closing about midnight. The evangelistic team came prepared with their power generators, and the place was ablaze with light and sound. Anyone who didn't know where the event was held, could just follow the sound, heard for miles around.

Several of our mission team attended for an evening just to experience evangelistic strategy worlds apart from ours. After a couple hours of music and flimflam, the evangelist finally took the stage. He harangued the audience for over an hour with a message that could have been said in two sentences: "Accept Jesus into your heart and when you die you will go to heaven. In the meantime, as an act of good measure God will heal you of your back pain provided you have enough faith."

The evening's events, though a bit shabby around the edges, took me back to my childhood, when even Mennonites were bitten with the evangelistic crusading fervor. Hundreds of people came forward for healing and salvation at the extended-closing invitation. Counselors met and prayed with each respondent and took information for follow-up contact.

But a year later, after checking with some of the church leaders, I found that the number of people who actually affiliated with a church as a result of the campaign could be counted on one hand.

People living in the villages find this style of evangelism insulting and offensive. They want to hear the Gospel from people living among them rather than from hit-and-run evangelists. In the early years of the mission, as we would go out from Catel to share the Gospel in nearby villages, the people of the village would invariably ask if we were going to leave them. "No," we would say, "we live here, just a couple miles down the road in the village of Catel, and we are here to stay." The locals, accustomed to itinerant evangelists, assumed we were more of the same. There was a significant expectation of abandonment by the missionaries. Some villages had experienced numerous instances of missionaries coming to preach at them and immediately being forgotten when the missionaries moved on.

Living among them, we were able to take time to listen to their stories, their hopes and dreams for a better life. We assured them we were concerned for them, although we needed to be cautious not to create expectations for the instant development they dreamed about.

Living with the locals in the Cacheu region of northwest Guinea-Bissau, we gradually became aware of the complexity of their needs: spiritual, social, medical, nutritional and economic. As we got a better picture of their needs, we were able to propose ways that we would be able to work as servants alongside them to bring resolution and hope.

This servanthood, divine-presence, working-alongside model, puts the responsibility on them to resolve their problems, an option not easily or readily understood by the locals. They wanted ready-made, just-add-water-and-stir solutions. Such solutions are not sustainable and can easily deepen dependency and poverty. It actually takes years to help people see that they need to furnish the solutions to their problems, while our role is to be there as facilitators and encouragers for change.

To put it in its most succinct terminology, being a servant of Christ in this West African setting means that one is a divine presence, an incarnation, if you will, of God here in this location. This definition applies to cross-cultural missionaries as well as the in-culture disciples of Jesus that result from the Good News the missionaries have proclaimed. Everything a disciple of Jesus says, either in word or deed, must represent God's will and design for mankind and all of his creation. There is no way for this servant-disciple model to happen outside of being physically present with those one is attempting to reach.

A leader in the Catel church testified that an important factor in his decision to follow Jesus was the humility portrayed in the lifestyle of the missionaries. He said, "You came and lived with us and lived like us. We know that you left a very good life in North America to come and share the gospel with us; you did not hesitate to leave all those nice things behind and become like us. You invited us into your house, the door was always open to us, and you helped us in the many difficulties of life here in the village. I was impressed by your humility. As I was thinking about that," he continued, "I read Philippians 2 where it talks about the humility of Christ, how he left everything behind just to do God's will and bring us salvation. Seeing how the lives of the missionaries was parallel to that of Christ, for me, authenticated the message you were sharing with us."

The locally-made disciple of Jesus, once abiding in Christ and discipled to follow Christ, is actually far better prepared to represent God in his native culture than is the cross-cultural missionary, although it takes the cross-cultural to get the process initiated and sustained. Attempting to be this divine presence in a foreign culture is fraught with numerous obstacles and potential flaws, but as the old saw goes, somebody has to do it. Someone needs to be the sent one; otherwise the good seed and the good soil will never come together.

The divine presence, servanthood model takes into account where people are at, socially, materially, intellectually and spiritually, and it then projects a vision of where these people could be if living according to God's design.

The Community of Christ in a Culture of Poverty

A woman in Catel prepares to do the family laundry at a village well.

In the three countries where MCWA is active (Gambia, Senegal, and Guinea-Bissau), about 75 percent of the population lives on less than $2 per day. If you go to the metropolitan areas of these countries, you will see classy government buildings and high rise luxury apartment towers; a few people will be whizzing down palm-lined boulevards in their shiny Toyota Land Cruisers on their way to a glitzy shopping center. When I pick up visitors at the Dakar airport and we drive through up-scale neighborhoods of the city, I need to tell them this is not the way it really is.

For the vast majority of West Africans that is not anything even close to reality. Most West Africans eke out a day-by-day existence doing whatever it takes to have a few coins to buy some rice and oil for their one meal per day. Most West Africans remain functionally illiterate and have no access to the medical care they need. Life expectancy for most people is under fifty years because of these harsh, deprived conditions.

After decades of high-powered, high-dollar development efforts, the chasm between the rich and poor in West Africa continues to deepen. Trickledown economics is a fantasy maintained by the elites as they capture more and more power and wealth.

MCWA is a church of the poor, for the poor, and by the poor. In the decades ahead that could change, but for the present and foreseeable future this is mostly what is on the menu.

Contrary to what Satan and wealth-oriented people would have us think, poverty is something we can rejoice about because according to Jesus it is the poor who are the blessed inheritors of God's kingdom. In Luke 6:2, Jesus says as he lifted up his eyes on his disciples: "Blessed are you who are poor, for yours is the kingdom of God." What a gift! What a blessing to be among the poor! We are part of God's kingdom! What more is there?

Conversely, the New Testament has words of woe and warning to those who are well off. To find some basis for affirmation of wealth, one needs to go back before the Jesus event into the

Old Testament. And even there the blessing of wealth is on fairly shaky terrain. Even in Old Testament days, God granted wealth with the expectation for it to be used to help the less fortunate. God never intended wealth for personal aggrandizement and for solidifying self-serving power.

In the kingdom of God we have it all: peace, security, love, hope, family, friends, community, and enough. That is why the community of Christ is so attractive to most people in poverty. That is why the church grows easily and quickly among the world's poor.

The problems and challenges of being a church of the poor are mostly the result of wanting to replicate the church as it is elsewhere in the settings of wealth over here in a setting of poverty. Somehow even the poor have picked up a vision for what church should be like from the North American models: a large, architecturally correct building, a salaried, professional staff of people to do the ministry, adjunct programs and institutions and whatever else it takes to make Christianity comfortable and progressive.

None of this is even on the screen for believers who don't have enough to eat, little or no medical care, and are illiterate and politically powerless. Thus we ask—how do we do church and what does church look like among the poor? First, what are we aiming for? How do we define the community of Christ? What is the baseline?

The community of Jesus' disciples is a visible group of persons committed to following the rule of Christ, the first and most important of which is to "love the Lord God with all our heart, soul and mind and our neighbor as ourselves." We live by the ethic of Jesus in all our relations; we are servants to each other and live life under the direction and power of the Holy Spirit. Our goal is to reflect the righteousness of God and, by our words and deeds, to invite others to join us in the family of God.

If that is an adequate definition of church, then the most important component of the church is the people who make up the body, each using their Spirit-empowered gifts to build up the body; enabling it to carry on the church's mission. And all that can be done without a dime. Thus, there should be no problem realizing a fully operational community of Christ even among the world's poorest people. The church to be church should have nothing to do with finances or the lack thereof.

But we have encountered a couple of significant challenges to being and doing church in a culture of poverty for which we have yet to find a solution.

If people are to develop their gifts that go into making church happen they need to be discipled. But when one is this poor, who has time to be discipled? People in poverty need nearly all their waking hours and energies to be focused on physical survival. Taking an afternoon off for Bible study and discipling is a luxury the poor can't afford. Subsistence agriculture requires one to work almost constantly. All labor is intensive, exhausting manual labor. Our people do not even have draft animals, let alone a tractor.

Many times when I have attempted to have evening Bible study, discipleship sessions, I am invariably looking at nodding heads and barely open eyelids. These guys are totally exhausted just trying to physically provide for their families. Sometimes they are just too tired even to show up. The poor know little about Sabbath, leisure or diversion. Just survive. We have yet to find a workable solution to discipling activities for believers living in the culture of poverty.

Another sticky wicket related to doing church in the culture of poverty is the meetinghouse question. Western missionaries have been coming to Africa for four centuries and one of the first things they do is to a build house where God lives and where we go to meet him. This fits well into African spirituality: God, if he is to be among us and part of our lives, obviously needs a place to live.

In the Balanta culture, it is the men's responsibility to till the soil. They use no animal traction for this work, only grub hoes and hand-operated plows.

My African friends have yet to figure out what's with these Mennonite missionaries who teach that God does not live in a building made by the hands of men. And we can meet him, worship him, and be with him anywhere and everywhere, even right here in the shade of this mango tree in our front yard. Oops! Now we have another problem. Under a tree? Ah, so you have a sacred tree where you meet your God? You must have borrowed a page from our animistic friends; that's where they do their cultic activities, under the shade of a sacred tree. Their spirit lives in that tree and they need to go there to communicate with him and ask for his help.

Well, maybe the meetinghouse option isn't so bad after all. We built the meetinghouse in Catel within the first year after arriving there. And it has been a good thing because in addition to providing a space for Sunday worship, we have used the facility for a multitude of ministry activities that go with being a holistic gospel mission. Everything imaginable happens in that space: clinic, pre-school, literacy classes, video theater, cashew storage and guesthouse to name just a few ministry activities we continually have there.

True, our evangelical church friends have been appalled at the array of profane things Mennonites do in God's house. But for us from the lived theology tradition our objective is not to create a holy space. Holy space is created anywhere and anytime we engage in doing God's will here on earth as it is already realized in heaven. Plus we get the most mileage out of the meetinghouse investment. In any case, the meetinghouse is clearly the winner up against the shade of a mango tree.

The Poverty Survival Kit

"Therefore I tell you, do not be anxious about your life, what you will eat or what you will drink, nor about your body, what you will put on. Is not life more than food, and the body more than clothing? Look at the birds of the air: they neither sow nor reap nor gather into barns, and yet your heavenly Father feeds them. Are you not of more value than they? And which of you by being anxious can add a single hour to his span of life? And why are you anxious about clothing? Consider the lilies of the field, how they grow: they neither toil nor spin, yet I tell you, even Solomon in all his glory was not arrayed like one of these.

But if God so clothes the grass of the field, which today is alive and tomorrow is thrown into the oven, will he not much more clothe you, O you of little faith? Therefore do not be anxious, saying, 'What shall we eat?' or 'What shall we drink?' or 'What shall we wear?' For the Gentiles seek after all these things, and your heavenly Father knows that you need them all. But seek first the kingdom of God and his righteousness, and all these things will be added to you" (Matthew 6:25-33).

In the Gospels much space is devoted to Jesus' judgment and warnings directed at the wealthy, the powerful, and the religious. But the essence of his presence and message of salvation is directed at the poor. In these verses Jesus directs the poor towards a conversion that refocuses and reorients life to establishing the reign and will of God. Jesus promises that if our focus is the ushering in of God's kingdom our physical and material needs will be met in the process.

Jesus isn't suggesting we piously sit with our hands folded and our eyes gazing up into the skies. He is saying that, as we relieve ourselves of anxiety about material things, rest in God's providential love for us and enter fully into the holistic community of Christ, together we will find adequate provision of material things.

Facilitating this conversion is the task of the missionary and pastoral leaders establishing community among the poor. We bring people together in God's kingdom where we learn how to develop and care for his creation in ways that will supply adequate sustenance for a full life.

The compass the poor have in finding their way out of poverty is themselves, joined together in a community seeking God's will to be done on earth as it is in heaven.

The Community of Christ in a Culture of Violence

When the Mennonite mission arrived in Catel in 2005, there was no organized church in the village. In fact, that is one of the reasons for selecting Catel as our center village. We soon discovered, however, that there was indeed a lay pastor in the village who had been attempting for some time to get a church going. However, he never managed much more than to gather a handful of children for Sunday school, singing and a sermon. Eight years later he was still trying but with scant results. This man was also a school teacher.

Sadly, one day he got into a conflict with one of his teacher colleagues at the school. When the row escalated to physical violence, the lay pastor inflicted serious injury to his opponent.

This to illustrate the significant difference it makes when the community of Christ has followed the Lord's example of relinquishing the personal aggrandizement model in favor of being the suffering servant who lays everything aside in favor of the advancement of God's kingdom. The acquisitive, possessive drive generates rivalry that can easily end in violence.

The Apostle Paul encourages us to imitate the servant, peace-making model of Jesus:

"Do nothing from rivalry or conceit, but in humility count others more significant than yourselves. Let each of you look not only to his own interests, but also to the interests of others. Have this mind among yourselves, which is yours in Christ Jesus, who, though he was in the form of God, did not count equality with God a thing to be grasped, but made himself nothing, taking the form of a servant, being born in the likeness of men. And being found in human form, he humbled himself by becoming obedient to the point of death, even death on a cross" (Philippians 2:3-8).

Though Jesus was tempted to do otherwise, he was faithful to the servant model the Father had ordained for him. Jesus never doubted the justice and right-making power of the Father. It is this same conviction and assurance that undergirds believers in West Africa. It enables them to be peacemakers in a violent society; it sustains them through their loss and suffering for Christ.

The Community of Christ Expects Suffering

Suffering for the sake of Christ happens because we, like him, confront the brokenness and marring of life apart from God in our families and villages with nonviolence and peace. The cross of Jesus, the cross which his disciples gladly take up, publically reveals the power and oppressiveness of evil. Evil assumes its own security and domination, but God, through the cross of Jesus and that of his disciples, disarms these powers and brings them to shame. "He disarmed the rulers and authorities and put them to open shame, by triumphing over them in him [Christ]" (Colossians 2:15).

The powers are not about to take this shame lying down. They are up in arms, mobilizing their forces, bringing persecution to believers willing to stand up to the evil of the powers that keep people bound to the destructive purposes of Satan. Therefore, suffering because we are followers of Jesus is both expected and normal. Suffering results because the dominating culture of darkness is threatened by the change brought by the values of God's kingdom.

Power brokers within the worldly value system resist defeat brought by the victorious, resurrected Messiah Jesus. Consequently, Jesus followers are offensive and will suffer persecution for upsetting worldly values. As we give witness to Christ and his kingdom, our alternate society, we can expect opposition and persecution. The true fellowships, the disciples of Jesus, are destined to suffer persecution just as Jesus did. It is through suffering that we are purified.

The kicker is that the opposition of the enemy is confronted on the terms of Christ rather than the weapons of the flesh used by the enemy itself. The kingdom of God relies on love and peacemaking to accomplish its ends rather than the exercise of violence, human power.

Yielding to God through submission to him and his desires for creation will inevitably produce suffering on the part of the followers of Jesus. Qualities of life in Christ are humility, patience, resignation and renunciation of wealth and earthly treasures, all of which hold the potential for suffering. Just dying to the domination of these things in our own lives causes pain.

How believers respond to opposition generated because of their witness against evil is particularly noted in the First Epistle of Peter. Messiah followers chose to resist the evil of the surrounding culture by suffering rather than mounting violent self-defense.

Laying down one's life as a disciple of Jesus, even to the point of martyrdom, provides us the opportunity to give witness to the power and logic of the death and resurrection of Christ. The peaceful sacrifice and suffering of Christians sow seeds for advancement of God's Kingdom.

Suffering with Christ and incarnating his compassion and love for the unlovely, the impure, the defiled and broken, will open the way for them to experience the redemptive work provided by Christ. In our transformation we participate in God's redemptive work by bridging the gaps between lostness and wholeness for all of God's creation.

Five years into our ministry in Catel, Guinea-Bissau, the Mennonite church was ready to commission some of the first disciples to go into neighboring villages to share the gospel. The villages were close enough that most of these men were known to the villagers to whom they were bringing the good news of Jesus.

One of the preachers returned to a village where he had previously been known as a man given to drunkenness, violence and womanizing. His friends in the village were incredulous at his transformation, and it took some time for them to accept that this was not the same person they had known five years earlier. His metamorphosis into a man of compassion, sobriety, peace, and purity came as a bit of a shock.

On one of his visits he arrived in a village and it was obvious there was a serious disturbance among the men. They were gathered at the house of the youth association leader with much animated conversation and shouting going on among themselves. He soon learned that the men were upset because two of the young women of the village had refused to attend a dance the previous night.

Village dance events are all-night affairs providing the young men opportunity for sexual encounters with their female age-group counterparts. But in stark contrast to this cultural expectation, the preacher had begun teaching a biblical vision for sexuality and marriage. Some of the young women were starting to catch the light of the Gospel and, consequently two of them refused to carry on the cultural expectation for single women. The men had met to determine how the two dissidents were to be punished.

The Good News bearer arrived at the God-appointed moment and intervened on behalf of the women, succeeding to convince the men not to carry out the sentence of punishment. He risked bringing punishment on himself for contradicting local custom, but he was successful in bringing peace and an important Gospel witness to the village. And in a broader view, the reign of God had brought light, again pushing back the darkness of the evil one.

Chapter 8

Confronting the Lies
of Animistic West Africa

First, a story: Binta is not a composite, representative fabrication but the real life experience of an actual person in our community of faith. Binta is her real name. As you read this story, I want you to imagine you are sitting with her on the veranda hearing her tell of what has been happening to her in recent days. As you enter into the pain, brokenness and hopelessness of her situation, you need to imagine how Jesus would be there with her to bring peace, comfort, hope, healing and wholeness to her. How would you be a facilitator for her salvation in its broadest, biblical sense? This is the challenge of being the community of Christ in the context of animistic West Africa.

Binta came to our clinic with a profusely bleeding big toe on her left foot. We wrapped it in gauze and sent her home telling her to keep it elevated and come for more bandaging once the bleeding had stopped. Binta is 29 years old, the mother to six children ages one to seven. Her injury occurred as she was preparing her rice field for planting. Toiling day after day in the hot sun, with ten-months-old James tied on her back, she was removing the weeds and grass from last year, hacking away at them with her 24-inch machete. It was hard work. We were seven months into

the dry season and the ground was like cement, but this is necessary preparation for the next rice crop.

This day, shortly before quitting the field to go home to
prepare the evening meal, the machete glanced off a clod of clay
and came down onto her left foot, splitting the toenail and cutting the flesh to the bone. When she realized what had happened,
she quickly tore off a strip of cloth and improvised a bandage.
Then she gathered her tools and lunch bowl and started limping
back to her house nearly a mile away, all the while with James
on her back.

Her injury brought great physical pain for her and additional
hardship to the family. Her husband, Gabriel, is the other half of
the breadwinning team, and it takes both working from daylight
to dark to provide even a small amount of food for the family
and keep a roof over their heads. Now, until healing comes to
her foot, she is unable to participate in the seasonal agricultural
tasks: soil preparation for the rice planting only two months away,
harvesting straw to re-thatch their roof against the coming rainy
season and gathering cashew nuts with the rest of the family.
This season of the year their daily rice is earned by turning in
two pounds of cashews in exchange for one pound of rice. All of
these activities are crucial for the well being of her family. But
now she was temporarily disabled.

Still, the blows didn't stop. Three days after the accident, she
learned that the land she was tilling for rice had been reassigned
by the village chief to someone else. Those six days of hard labor
on the soil were for naught. Now she will have to seek another
plot of land, if any is still available. That will not be easy. So life

goes on, day by day, not knowing if there will be food tomorrow or what reverses may still be coming.

Binta's extended family are refugees from neighboring Senegal. A clan of lawless bandits drove them from their village in Senegal where they had a home, land, enough to eat and a school for their children. They took refuge about fifteen miles away in Guinea-Bissau. Here, because of their refugee status, their rights are significantly curtailed. It was not unexpected that their rice land should be taken by a Catel native. As refugees, they are without recourse. Many times they have been subjected to harassment and humiliation by long-term residents. Although they are from the same tribe as the local people, they belong to a different subgroup within the tribe.

The Mane family is active in the Catel Mennonite Church. Binta had not yet been baptized since her faith was still in an early stage, but she is making good progress. Gabriel, because he is fluent in French, was able to study the Bible and interact freely with me. His faith is maturing quickly, and his primary goal is the evangelization of his family.

Yet, another heartache is that two of their children from a previous relationship, Nau and Ramatoulai, have cleft palates, likely caused by inadequate nutrition for the mother during the first three months after conception. There is little hope for corrective surgery in this land where medical care is scant and the parents have no way to cover medical costs.

As Binta's story trails off into silence, you are still there with her and she is waiting for your words and deeds that will help her experience the deliverance, wholeness, and transformation that accompanies the salvation of Messiah Jesus. What will your ministry to her look like? How do we bring the saving work of Christ to the pain and sorrow of a life like Binta's?

Salvation: Understanding the Mission of Messiah Jesus

There are numerous ways we understand the saving work of Jesus Christ, all of which significantly shape the way we live the Christian life and the way we do mission. These saving motifs are particularly important in describing the Anabaptist understanding of atonement, that is, how mankind and all of creation are being transformed and put right with God.

First, we understand God, in the form of the man Jesus, came to earth to live the life of an ordinary person, except that in his life he was utterly and totally faithful to God. He lived the life of an ordinary man without sin, in perfect obedience to the will of the Father. His astonishing faithfulness to God exploded the myth of Satan's earthly power. His resurrected presence left Satan a helpless, bound, powerless wimp. Jesus, with his approaching death in view, draws the final curtain on Satan's domain. In John 12:31 he announces, " Now is the judgment of this world; now will the ruler of this world be cast out."

In Jesus' day, people generally assumed that the Messiah would come as a charismatic, powerful, triumphant warrior, but instead he came as a suffering servant. His overcoming weapon was suffering love, even unto death.

Living in complete fulfillment of God's desire for man, the Christ did not suffer the consequences of sin, eternal death. He broke the ultimate power of Satan over mankind through his resurrection into life eternal with God. In this, he became the firstfruit of what all of us can become. Through our faithfulness to him, we share in his victory over the power and the curse of Satan in our lives. In our mission here, we participate with him in the plundering of the kingdom of Satan. When this life is over, we will share his glorious life in the eternal eschatological kingdom of God.

Of first importance for us today is how we share in the power of his resurrection already in this life as we also die to our sinful natures, behaviors and desires. In that process, we are already raised to newness of life, joined to Christ. His new life of the Spirit within us enables us to live faithfully and righteously, rec-reated into the image of God. While we become neither God nor perfect, he does adopt us as his own children who naturally take on the qualities, character and likeness of our Father.

The church then is a company of adopted children, looking and acting like their Father. The church is a discipled community living under the rule of Christ and imitating him in his suffering, sacrifice, servanthood, and his submission to the Father.

The significance of an entire community of people living life in freedom from the power of Satan is expressed as the kingdom of God on earth, wherein God's righteousness dwells and is made manifest to all of creation. The Spirit's power and presence within and among us transform our material reality. The established life of the community of Christ portrays God's new order of righteousness, justice and peace which he originally planned for his creation.

Revelation 21:5 tells us that God is making all things new. The church believes the process of making all things new had its inauguration on earth with the cross and the empty tomb of Christ two millennia ago. The church, as we understand it, significantly embodies the new things God is doing in his world. As such, the ministry of the church must be fully engaged in the ongoing task of making all things new by addressing all the areas of human existence and brokenness. It is from this platform of understanding the mission of Messiah Jesus that we are equipped to minister to the multitudes of Bintas in West Africa.

Gibby Mane, a leader in the Mennonite congregation, stands in a forestry project at the Mission.

The witness and life of the community of Christ point to a new way of life destined to replace all other ways of life. Therefore, the ministry of the church critiques all aspects of the cultural, social, and economic context by the way it lives and witnesses in word, deed, and worship. The church is an alternative society because it portrays life in the coming, fulfilled kingdom of God. If this vision is absent in a church, it is because the church has been compromised and conformed to this world, (Romans 12:1). When that happens, the church is merely a reflection of the fallen creation in which it finds itself.

Our life together here on earth is a foretaste of God's eternal eschatological community. In this community we have practices and attitudes that are more at home in the next age, the consummated kingdom of God, than they are in this age. The church is redeemed and its actions are in the direction of the redemption of others and all of creation. We are eager to see the establishment of God's new order of righteousness, justice and peace.

This view of salvation, so prominent in the first century of the church, is known as the Christus victor motif. Because of the close parallels between first century culture and that of West Africa, this motif is equally meaningful and of first importance to new believers there. Both cultures are/were in bondage to the gods of this world: Satan, demons, witchcraft, ancestral spirits and men claiming divinity.

Life in a culture like that means the majority of people will live lives similar to that of Binta. Only a tiny minority (the powerful, wealthy elites), will attain an illusory "good" life. The rest of the population will live in misery, poverty, sickness, fear, violence and sadness.

There are other significant Scriptural atonement motifs: substitutionary sacrifice, purchase-redemption, the suffering servant and liberation, among others. In this case I simply lift up the Christus victor motif because seekers in an animistic culture find it their most logical and appealing entre into God's kingdom.

When Messiah becomes present in culture—any culture, he is bound to bring transformation to people and their worldview. There is release from captivity, joy, celebration, peace, healing and well-being. There is the formation of a new community, a new peoplehood characterized by love, forgiveness, caring and servanthood. It happened in the first century in the primitive apostolic church and is happening again today in West Africa and many other regions of the global South. It needs to be happening far more in the North than what most of us can even imagine or are even open to.

Nor would I suggest that becoming a Christian in an animistic culture is somehow easy. It is not. There is all manner of opposition to those who begin to turn toward Jesus and follow as disciples. There is great social pressure upon those who give up their place in the demonic scheme of the now and the next life.

Cultural values and worldview have their origins in one of two places: Either they grow out of a relation of faithfulness to the Creator God and his design for creation or they are derived from the fallenness of mankind following the evil powers of this world dominated by Satan.

When people chose to follow Satan's rebellious, contra God's design, they have given Satan permission to establish strongholds within the culture. Satanic strongholds exist in all cultures, some more, some less.

The missionary task, understood at its most basic, is to proclaim, invite and facilitate the establishment of God's kingdom, settings where his will is being done on earth, as it is in heaven. God's rule is established as satanic strongholds are destroyed and people begin living in the reality of God's new creation.

Strongholds happen when people take for granted (believe) the lies of Satan. The stronghold allows Satan full freedom to do what he does best: kill, steal and destroy. The goal of the Mennonite mission in West Africa is to walk with Africans towards the recovery of God's design and to help the emerging church in its establishment of God's reign in this corner of his creation.

The satanic lies found in West Africa form an interwoven web that holds animistic Africans in a powerful bondage of blindness and hopelessness that only the life, death and resurrection of Christ is able to break. By way of illustration, I will list four of the most prevalent satanic lies in Guinea-Bissau along with some of the evidences and consequences of the lies in the lives and communities of our mission. Following that, I have listed some of the practical Gospel transformations believers are experiencing as they begin to follow Jesus. These transformations normally aren't overnight phenomena. They are incremental lifestyle/worldview changes as the light and truth of Christ become recognized and embraced.

Lie 1: Women and children are of less value than men.

- Women are the property of men. As little girls grow up, they are household slaves, seldom getting an education and always busy working around the compound doing menial tasks. Even at age ten, girls can be sold to a much older man as a "wife." She may not actually live with him at that age but she has been promised to him and her father has received compensation for her. When a man has sexual relations with a woman (and this always happens before marriage) and she becomes pregnant with his child, she is still under the domination of her father and brothers until her partner has paid the full amount being asked for her by her father. Being faithful to one spouse is practically unheard of; it is not perceived as a value. Sex is for wherever and with whomever you can have it.

- Women are valued for labor and procreation. A couple is not held together in a caring, romantic and mutually fulfilling relationship. They are together to bear children who will care for them in their old age and assure their passage into the ancestral spirit world. Husbands and wives maintain totally separate agendas and circles of friends. There is always the fear that an unhappy spouse will put a curse on the partner as a revenge for an injustice or offense.

- Generally children are properly cared for within the limits of abject poverty, but in their developing years it is rare for a child to be raised by both

The African women are generally very enterprising. Here a Catel woman is recovering salt from the tidal flats close to the village. The salt can be sold at the local markets.

biological parents. It is also unusual to see a parent engaging in playful, affectionate interaction with the child. Most children are born and raised in a setting of step-siblings who have diverse parental care, and there is often severe competition and favoritism. Children are easily passed from household to household. Corporal punishment is harsh and frequent, always administered in a context of parental anger.

Let me share the story of Ramatoula, not at all an exception to the way children are treated in West Africa even by people who call themselves Christian:

The little girl dressed in a dirty, tattered T-shirt, probably six years old and barely 36-inches tall, moved noiselessly into my door frame, after dark, on the evening of April 30, 2011. I can still see this little waif standing there, not saying a word, a blank face but fear in her eyes.

That day had not started off well for Ramatoula. As daylight was stealing across the Guinea-Bissau landscape and the roosters were about done with their morning announcements, another song was heard in the house of Ramatoula's caregiver. It was the voice of her auntie, who had taken custody of this child from Ramatoula's mother three weeks earlier. The auntie was singing a ditty about a little girl who again wet the bed and needed to be punished. The song and the accompanying ruckus awakened one of our missionary co-workers.

When he heard Ramatoula's screams, he quickly leaped from his bed and dashed out to the veranda where the goings-on sickened and angered him. There was this little half-pint being held inside an empty rice sack. Around her was the rest of the household doing a mock lynching on her.

"Bring a machete" said her auntie, "we need to cut her up." A machete was brought and one of the men began sharpening it on the cement blocks.

More Screams and Wailing from the Rice Sack

"We will throw her down the well," said one of the men, laughing at Ramatoula's anguish.

My co-worker began challenging the group, telling them it is child abuse and they needed to stop. The auntie became angry at him, saying he should not interfere with their disciplining of the child. "This is the only way African children can learn to stop doing things they shouldn't do," said the auntie. I have heard that reasoning many times in West Africa. On several occasions I have told people that when the child is "flogged," as they call it, he learns only two things: 1) the guy who hits the hardest is the winner, and 2) the best way to control others is by violence.

As she stood in my doorway that evening, Ramatoula's troubled eyes were pleading for affection and security. Seeing little children suffer is one of the toughest parts of being a missionary in West Africa.

Ramatoula is one of millions of unwanted, uncared for, abandoned children in this part of the world. Her father is a witch doctor with multiple wives and partners. Her mother, who is pregnant with another child and unable to care for Ramatoula, had dropped her off at the auntie's house.

I'm not telling this story for the shock value, I am telling it to help us be aware of the great challenge before us as the church emerges and grows in West Africa. EMM missionaries have our work cut out for us.

The perpetrators in this incident, specifically the auntie, are professing Christians. She even labels herself a missionary and leads worship at her church. That children must not be abused and disciplined like this is news even for believers.

I am in Africa to invite people to become disciples of Jesus, that is, to give the Holy Spirit permission to begin transforming them into a new creation that will look and act like Jesus. But it's not necessary for me to invite Ramatoula; she's already there (see Mark 10:14).

Meeting Ramatoula has helped me hone my mission vision in four ways:

1. I would like to help people view the world and others the way God sees us/them. Psalm 82:3 tells us God expects his people to "Give justice to the weak and the fatherless; maintain the right of the afflicted and the destitute."

2. I would like to help people find the way of peace as they live with each other, learning that violence and forceful coercion only give birth to more of the same.

3. I would like to teach parenting skills enabling parents to raise children to know they are loved and valued and to start a revolution in the way we do family.

4. I would like to help people (and myself) to know that the little Ramatoulas are the greatest in the kingdom of heaven, and to be a part of that kingdom, each of us needs to become a Ramatoula.

The lies about gender, family life, and marriage were not always this bad in West Africa. In the early years of the twenty-first century there were still grandmothers in our area of West Africa who could recall the days of their youth when everyone in their particular ethnic group believed and practiced that sex happened only between a man and his wife after they had been publicly married. Fornication and adultery were taboo and carried the stigma of social shame in this pre-Christian traditional tribal society.

It was an example of what Paul describes in Romans 2:14-15: " For when Gentiles, who do not have the law, by nature do what the law requires, they are a law to themselves, even though they do not have the law. They show that the work of the law is written on their hearts, while their conscience also bears witness, and their conflicting thoughts accuse or even excuse them."

Prior to the 1970s, when a young man desired to have a particular woman as wife, he never met privately with her or in a setting where they would have had opportunity for sexual relations. Sex was consummated only after they were publicly joined as a couple. The marriage was initiated when a son told his father of his desire for a particular woman. His dad would send one of his own brothers (uncle of the prospective groom), to the young woman's dad to begin discussion of the possible marriage.

Today much of that tradition has changed. Marriages are still arranged by the groom's family, and the dowry is still given, but nowadays the bride-to-be is typically, already pregnant and needing to get married to the father of her child. Sexual relations prior to marriage are common even among evangelical Christians. Adulterous relations are likewise common among non-Christians but forbidden of Christians.

Traditional marriage among ethnic groups in West Africa has included a significant element of mistrust in marriage and gender relations. The tribal power secrets, including the power of death curses to an enemy and the enlistment of the ancestors for protection, is a spiritual power system of knowledge to be known and passed down only by the males of the tribe, village or clan. These secrets must not be allowed to come into the knowledge of females, especially one's wife or daughters. Boys going through coming of age rites are taught these secrets and take death vows if they ever share them with a female, including one's wife. If the wife knows the husband's tribal secrets and demonic compacts, she will share them with her clan, her first loyalty. Once the secrets are known by another clan, the spirit powers can be neutralized and overcome by the enemy.

However, there is a vision among evangelical leaders, including those in the Mennonite community, to establish a norm for marriage as a publically acknowledged joining of one man and one woman into a lifelong, covenanted relationship of sacrificial love, mutual trust and care of each other. Sexual relations happen only between a man and a woman who have made this public commitment to each other as husband and wife. This goal encompasses a broad canvas of gender relations and family life that includes romance, mutual submission, the equality of men and women and nurturing Christ-like care for children who are born into this family.

Reestablishing that ideal is not going to be easy and will require much grace and discipline among faithful followers of Jesus. Leaders among both men and women will need to be models for biblically-based ideals for marriage. These principles will need to be taught to children throughout their time in the parental home.

How the Gospel Light Transforms this Lie

1. There is a growing mutuality in the marriage relationship and in the one-flesh understanding. Each partner shares in child rearing, household work and family finances. There is a growing sense of care and responsibility for others in the immediate and extended family. There is mutual submission

within the family, although men continue to exercise servant oriented leadership for the family.

2. Being faithful to your spouse is news to most of these people. But there is openness to the concept of faithfulness as it reflects the character of God. Faithfulness between spouses becomes an extension of the Son's faithfulness to his Father God and God's faithfulness towards mankind and all his creation. Faithfulness also belongs to the relationship among the brothers and sisters of Christ: our new family, our new identity and our new story. Faithfulness is a quality of all relationships when one is a disciple of Jesus.

3. People are precious. Life is a gift from God. We begin to realize our responsibility to help those who are poor, marginalized, ill and in trouble. We see others as worthy recipients of God's grace and transforming power. We have a vision for the possibilities of holistic salvation in everyone we are in touch with.

Lie 2: People are created to be dominated and manipulated by one who is stronger; each, in turn, looks below to find those he is able to relate with through dominance.

People are generally friendly and open with each other. Most visitors from outside the village or country are cordially received. It is a major offense not to greet people you meet along the way. But some times what starts out as friendly greeting quickly escalates into a power discussion with high pitch, angry decibels and broad, exaggerated accusations. Truth is unimportant; anything can be said. Often as people are engaged in a verbal aggression to dominate, they both are talking (shouting) at each other at the same time. There is an attempt to overpower and bully the other one with a stream of loud, dominating verbiage. But in the end, after ten minutes of animated back and forth, the parties are again engaging in friendly badgering. Beneath these animated exchanges and camaraderie there is only a veneer of trust.

There is a significant loyalty to tribe and village. In the recent past, inter-village raids were a way of life and still happen, particularly against villages across the border in Senegal. Thievery is not unusual, and always happens after dark. There is nothing terribly wrong with stealing; the most serious infraction is getting caught. Thieves are beaten, even fatally, if caught, provided they have not already been shot red-handed. The only protection against severe punishment is to flee to an army or police post. Even there corporal punishment will likely happen, and there will be no due process for a criminal.

There is a need to dominate, control and even destroy others through the use of curses, fetishes and demonic powers. Elaborate rituals, offerings and satanic consultations are staged in an effort to win the aid of demons, spirits and ancestors for protection against evil. If one is sick, it means an enemy has stolen his soul. If he has an accident, crop failure or an unsuccessful business venture, it means someone has put a curse on him. He is then obligated to consult the witchdoctor to find out who is responsible and what action must be taken not only to diffuse the power, but also to impose an even heavier disaster on his enemy.

In the drive to dominate, physical violence is always an easy option. Children learn this before they are two years old. It is common to see a small child walk up to a playmate and punch or shove him, totally without provocation. Adults settle scores with fists, sticks or machetes. It is important to hit harder and do more damage to the opponent than he initially did to you.

How the Gospel Light Transforms this Lie

1. Following the example of Jesus, disciples imitate their teacher by becoming servants rather than masters. They learn that God's objectives are sooner accomplished by servitude than by power and domination. Disciples die to their own wishes and objectives and join Jesus in his prayer, "Not my, but your will be done." Believers realize they are now part of a community voluntarily and joyfully resigned to accomplishing the Father's mission in the world.

2. With that issue settled, disciples of Jesus defer to the justice and judgment of God to settle wrongs. We no longer need to repay evil for evil; we see the will of God being done by blessing rather than cursing the wrongdoer. Unbelievers have been moved by the humility, grace and wisdom of Christians sooner than by brute force.

3. Jesus' followers are led by a strong eschatological assurance that in the end God dominates, that rewards and justice lie ahead and that losses now will be amply compensated in God's future.

4. Believers transition from putting curses on their enemies to forgiving them, praying for them and doing deeds of loving

service as a way of extending God's grace into the life of the enemy.

Lie 3: In the Spirit world, God is present but Satan is the preferred deity.

For the animistic practitioner, the spirit world is equally as real as the visible world. Of all the beings in the spirit world, none is more present and available than Satan and his minions. Satan is called upon for direction in decisions, protection from harm and guidance into the next world. God is there but he is less involved and less apt to carry out one's wishes.

This religion has a long list of ceremonies, sacred objects and cultic activities. People travel far and wide to patronize a renowned witchdoctor to guide them through all the hoops and myriad possibilities utilizing evil powers. The powers, skills and feats of a particular witch-doctor are passed by word of mouth from community to community, thereby generating faith in him.

People enter into contracts with demons enlisting the demonic power to carry out an evil scheme. The contracts require the client to give the soul of an innocent individual, usually a child, to meet the contractual agreement with the demon.

A daily chore is sweeping the yard surrounding the compound. In the lower left is a small grass hut where food or wine is offered to the ancestral spirits who are believed to inhabit the compound where they once lived.

Fear is the primary fruit of animism. The animist practitioner lives in constant fear of what others, both seen and unseen will do to him. It is assumed that the other's agenda is evil. No one is to be trusted; one's plans, wealth and advantages need to be shrouded in secrecy for fear that someone will intervene to steal or destroy.

How the Gospel Light Transforms this Lie

1. Africans are attracted to power sources. (Maybe that's characteristic of most people.) Christus victor is understood as a greater power than Satan because in his life as a man Jesus, not Satan, was in control. Satan was unable to persuade Jesus into falling for the satanic scheme of things. Jesus was unwavering in his commitment and obedience to God's plan. Even when Jesus became the victim of Satan-orchestrated death, he did not remain in the world of the dead. Jesus, as a man of flesh, broke the bondage of death and was transformed into an eternally new creation because he is the very author and source of life. Thus Satan's power has been marginalized and made of no effect in the life of the disciple of Jesus, an individual born of the Spirit of Christ.

2. Africans (as do all of us) become liberated, are set free from, and move beyond the power of Satan through the new life of Christ within.

3. African believers give up their consultations with purveyors of witchcraft and the cultic practices attempting to maneuver fate. They turn instead to the protection, care and direction of the Holy Spirit who lives in the heart of the believer.

4. Protection, care, and guidance are found in the community of believers who are made wise to God's will and are gifted to help each other as we live surrounded by powers of the evil one.

Lie 4: Africa's land and people are cursed, incapable of sustainable management and development. Success, prosperity, and technological progress are the domain of the white man.

The people of Guinea-Bissau, one of Africa's poorest and most undeveloped countries, see little beauty and well-being when they look around their environment. Everywhere are sickness, death, poverty and brokenness. Nothing works: the health system, infrastructure, government, education and agriculture. The only hopeful spots are those where white folks are part of the picture. Where white folks are not present, you can expect there will be corruption, mismanagement, and failure. We must depend on the outside to rescue/save us.

How the Gospel Light Transforms this Lie

This lie is difficult to deal with because it is so insidious. Everywhere you look, you see brokenness and dysfunction. And to reinforce the lie, most things that white people do will succeed, if they can do the job adequately isolated from the forces that pull things apart.

Why are things this broken? I attribute it to the all-pervading power of Satan in the region. Where Satan is called upon regularly and given full rein, he does what he is best at: wreaking havoc, destroying relationships and spreading fear and mistrust.

As people become believers and join in with the community of Christ, there is transition to orderliness, honesty, transparency, living by the rules, faithfulness, dying to self and ordering life

Rice plants in the nursery bed will be transplanted to the rice paddies.

by creator God's design. Where these believers live, move and have their being, life looks very different from the surrounding chaos of a Satan-dominated society. Among the believers, their lives, while not perfect, become showcases for justice, righteousness, harmony, peace, adequacy, health and success.

Truth Wins in Tening's Life

We started this chapter with a story; we end it with a testimony of transformation by Tening Mane. He shared it with me about five years after he first began turning towards Jesus. During that period he made a clear commitment to Christ and was baptized. He subsequently became a church leader, took nurse's training, and became a certified nurse. He is the director for the mission's health ministry. This is his story:

The most important part of my house was the front door. There at the entrance to the house was the habitation of the spirits of our ancestors. We cautiously passed there, firmly believing that they had great power over our lives and it was our obligation to stay on good terms with them.

Every year at the beginning of the rainy season in West Africa, we would assemble our agricultural tools (hoes, mattocks, machetes and shovels), and lean them up against the doorposts. There we would say to the ancestors and Satan, "Here we are, ready to start cultivating and planting the soil ahead of the rain. We are asking you to grant us plenty of rain, protection from thieves and insects and give us a good harvest." At the end of the harvest six months later, we would again gather around the door and thank the ancestors for providing our food for the months ahead. On both occasions there would be offerings of alcohol or animal blood poured out to seal our devotion to the ancestors. Failure to thank them would certainly result in sickness or other misfortune.

When we experienced hardship, sickness or disaster, we would immediately go to the witchdoctor asking his help to know who put a curse on us and what sort of counter measures we need to take to protect ourselves and how to repay and visit an even greater misfortune on our enemy. Our curse on the enemy would be sealed with an offering of a rooster or goat. The witchdoctor would give us an armband with a verse from the Koran in tiny pieces sealed in the amulet. This fetish gave us protection from evil. At other times, the witchdoctor would write the verse in ink on a paper, then wash out the ink in a small amount of water, and we would rub that water all over our bodies for protection against the evil.

Whenever there was a death, we were obliged to go to the witchdoctor to find out who put a curse on our family member, bringing about their demise. This involved many ceremonies and the expenditure of money to make the determination and put a counter-curse on the enemy.

Before marrying a woman, it was necessary to consult the witchdoctor to know if the marriage would be successful, that there would be children and that the woman would fill her proper role of submission.

The marginalization of women is one of the worst lies in our culture. All the work around the house, the farm and child rearing, is the responsibility of the woman. She must always offer great respect to her husband, waiting on him hand and foot. If she makes a mistake, she is brutally punished; there is no forgiveness, pity or affection.

Another heavy lie we live with is the belief that as African males, we are inferior and less intelligent than our white counterparts. When we look up at the sky and see the huge planes flying effortlessly above, we say, "See, the white man can make anything happen." When we go for medicine, we want it to come from the hand of a white man, not an African. When the gospel is preached, it is more believable and powerful preached by a white man.

All these things and much more were part of my worldview. I never doubted any of it. I was totally unaware there was another very different other reality.

That was what I believed until 2005 when EMM missionaries came to our village in Guinea-Bissau and began telling us about Jesus. We had no idea there was even a Messiah. We knew there was God, but we didn't know he had defeated Satan.

Through the knowledge of Jesus, I began to realize the presence of God all around me, that he loves me and that it was to him I owe my worship, obedience and faithfulness, not to the things that he had created. I learned that I, likewise, had been created in the image of God. I began to realize that all this witchcraft, sorcery and lies were what Satan was using to keep me and my people in total darkness.

In our instruction from the Bible, I learned that it is God alone who has all power over all his creation. I turned my heart towards God and began to leave the shadows and come into the light. I was all too happy to leave behind the horrors of slavery to Satan. All these demonic ceremonies, sacrifices, witchdoctors, sacred sticks and fears I rejected as lies of Satan. I have left all these and replaced them with faith in the Living God.

I am seeing in my heart and attitudes love towards those who would do evil to me. I am able to forgive those who do wrong to me, and I want to share God's grace with them instead of returning evil upon them.

Now I know that God has a beautiful design for a man and woman together in marriage. Anger towards my wife has been replaced with an intense love, and I know that God wants me to have only one woman to whom I am always faithful. I know that we have been created to be caring and committed to each other. I enjoy helping her with work around the compound like splitting wood, drawing water and cooking. I know we share mutually in the troubles and sufferings of life.

I know that God has created me with great intelligence to care for his creation and to get from creation the things we need to maintain a good life. He has created me to know how to distinguish good from evil.

Every day I thank him for the new life he has given us, and I look forward to continuing my walk with him.

The Faith Itinerary: We All Have One

I try to imagine what my own faith journey would have looked like had I been born in the Galilee region of Palestine some 2000 years ago. This is what I hope it might have been: As a thirteen-year-old, my friends and I were among a crowd of people listening to an itinerant teacher not unlike others who occasionally passed through my hometown, Capernaum. His name was Jesus, son of Joseph from Nazareth. But he was different from the other preachers.

He taught us things about God I had never thought about before, like the story of a father whose son disgraced the family name by wasting the family inheritance and living a very immoral life in a far country. But one day the son returned, and his dad received him back into the family, restoring the son's dignity and honor he had trashed a few months earlier. He told us that is what God is like, ready to receive us back into his family even though our lives were far different from what he wanted them to be. He taught with great authority, and I began to think in my heart and mind that what he taught came from God. This man was a like an old-time prophet.

Not only that, I personally knew people who were healed by him: sight was given to the blind, people who could scarcely move threw away their crutches and were walking and active like the rest of us, and one woman's son was brought back from the dead at Jesus' command.

Some people in Capernaum wondered out loud if this man could be the promised Messiah. Others said no, that the Messiah would need to drive out the Romans, setting us free from their pagan ways. He would need to be our God-appointed King, living at the Jerusalem palace and restoring the glory of Israel to what it was under King David.

He actually did go to Jerusalem saying that he was sent from God to establish God's kingdom. However, it wasn't the sort of kingdom our leaders were anticipating, and they wrote him off as an imposter, a fake messiah. They got the Romans to crucify him as an example to other so-called messiahs. It made the Romans happy to know our leaders were helping them keep order in Jerusalem.

That was last year. But now two or three men are in Capernaum, people who had been close disciples of Jesus. They are saying that Jesus did die, but three days later he was again seen alive. They themselves saw him and talked to him. His body was somehow changed; he was visible to them but he was also more like a spirit. They are proclaiming that he was indeed God's anointed Messiah. I am attending their meetings and I like what I am hearing. In my heart I am becoming more and more convinced that, indeed, this man Jesus was God's Son sent to inaugurate God's kingdom. I believe he is calling me to become part of those who know and worship him as Messiah Jesus.

That really wasn't my faith journey, but I am ruminating that it could have been something like that had I been born a couple thousand years earlier in far away Palestine. My real faith journey is in chapter one of this book.

That faith journey has taken me to West Africa where I am like those early apostles who returned to Capernaum to tell the people that, yes indeed, Jesus is God's anointed Messiah and he is inviting you to join us in the Christ-following community.

Here in West Africa, I share the good news about how Jesus can recreate our lives, heal us from the damaging power of satanic lies, give us hope for the future, relieve us from the cycle of curses and violence, create relationships of dignity between men and women, and much more as we are brought into God's family. As that message enters into the hearts and minds here, I ponder again how the Holy Spirit works, convicting and convincing people that, yes, the Jesus we talk about really is God's Messiah, and creating desire to become a disciple of Jesus, part of his community of faith.

Faith itineraries, whether in the context of first-century Jewish Palestine, twentieth-century North American Mennonite culture or a twenty-first century West Africa animistic culture, have a common denominator. In all those experiences, one moves from traditional beliefs, to gaining new information about Messiah Jesus, to sensing a need to be in relationship with him and, finally, to a resolve to open one's life to this Messiah Jesus, ready to sacrifice anything, including one's own life, just to be part of who he is and what he does for those who become part of God's new people.

In John 7:17, Jesus says to the skeptics: "If anyone's will is to do God's will, he will know whether the teaching is from God or whether I am speaking on my own authority." Those seeking faith in Jesus must come to a point of resolution (yes, this teaching of Jesus is from God, it is the eternal truth of God), and to willingness to do whatever it takes to be part of that truth.

The cultural, historical, psychological, and social settings where the Gospel is articulated in word and deed, can be vastly different, but there is a common faith itinerary as one moves his life, his spirit, and his thinking along the way to becoming a disciple of Jesus.

Discipleship can be described as spiritual union with Jesus and everything Jesus is about in our world and the entire cosmos, both in time and eternity. It's the "abiding" Jesus is talking about in John 15 with his allegory of the vine. The disciple abides in God and God abides in the disciple in relationship and commitment that supersede all others.

This relationship is intellectual and doctrinal, as in loving the Lord your God with all your heart, soul and mind, and it is equally ethical as one lives life in total obedience to the commandments of Christ subsumed under the dominant rule of love.

A missionary is one who invites, facilitates and encourages people to become disciples of Jesus. He assists and enables people along the way of their faith itinerary. The Mennonite mission has a goal to disciple Africans, enabling them to continue the work of calling and making disciples the way Jesus did during his ministry among us 2000 years ago.

Chapter 9

In Retrospect

In retrospect, I can more clearly see two additional underlying ways that God equipped me for pioneer work in Africa. As I wrote in Chapter 1, I identify with the Bible story about the lad who offers his loaves and fish to Lord. The lunch appears useless relative to the multitude of people needing to be fed, but Jesus multiplies our most meager offerings. From some perspectives, the two additional ways, which I refer to as Barley Loaf 4 and 5, may not seem as if they are much to offer. But, these two pieces are a vital part of my life's puzzle that God used to enable me to fulfill the special calling in my life.

Barley Loaf 4: Health

In childhood and on into adulthood, I was dogged by allergies and consequent respiratory problems. This seriously limited me in terms of physical activity, and I was constantly trying to avoid exposure to allergens. During those years, medical research and treatment of respiratory problems was still in its infancy, with few options for relief from acute asthma. In the mid-1970s I became a resident of the Willamette Valley in Oregon, and there I found some relief because ragweed, my most potent allergen, was not present. Still, the chilly, damp northwest winters made me subject to prolonged bouts of bronchitis. It wasn't until I left North America in January 2000 and took up permanent residence in Africa that I was delivered from all respiratory problems. In Africa I did not so much as catch a respectable cold.

It took me a few months of living in Africa to build up resistance to dysentery, but since then I have been virtually illness free. During my first six months in Africa, I did have one bout with malaria, but that served only to provide me with immunity to malaria, not a bad immunity to have on a continent where this infectious disease is the leading cause of death.

If I want to be ill, all I need to do is go back to North America, and sure enough, in less than a week I am experiencing shortness of breath and bronchitis. I enjoy visiting in North America, but I need to be on respiratory medication. When I return to the U.S., I make a ritual visit to the medical center for a checkup. Of the fifty or so tests done through blood work (cholesterol, sugar, PSA, etc.), usually everything is within the normal range. I asked a doctor how often people in their seventies have nearly perfect blood work. He replied, "It's almost unheard of."

In 2007 I did have a close call with a heart problem. I was in the U.S. for six weeks, and the director at Eastern Mennonite Missions (EMM), Clair Good, suggested that I have a stress test. I was having no problems or symptoms; nevertheless, I scheduled a stress test and sure enough my heart's transverse artery was blocked. The doctor called it an asymptomatic blockage, the sort where you don't know you have a problem until a heart attack strikes. I needed a stent as soon as possible.

The next problem was scheduling the surgery, since I was close to the departure flight back to Africa. I told the Heart Group I was available for stent surgery any time. On a Thursday before the Monday of my return flight, the hospital called to say they had a cancellation. An hour later I was in surgery and the titanium stent was slithered up through the proper arteries to the blocked transverse. The plaque was dispersed and the released stent completed the repair job. Much to the chagrin of the surgeon, three days later, I was on the flight to Dakar, Senegal. No problem.

All this good health the Lord has blessed me with in no way obscures my mortality. There isn't the least doubt in my mind that one day the Lord is going to say, "Well, you've done what I planned for you and now it's time for you to come home." And with that I will die in whatever circumstance the Lord already knows about.

And speaking of circumstances, I have one more story to share from my health and well-being files. One of the greatest risks faced by expatriates living in Africa is getting into a vehicle and traveling the highways. Traffic accidents in Africa are carnage unparalleled anywhere else in the world. Several EMM missionaries and church leaders have been touched by highway tragedies. I have traveled thousands of miles on African highways, both as a driver and as a passenger in public transportation and have never been in a highway accident. On several occasions I have been within inches and seconds of disaster, saved only by God's protective angels.

The chances of highway disaster in Africa are greatly multiplied for two reasons. One, most public transport vehicles are brought in after they have served their useful life in a developed country. Africa is the great dumping ground for whatever is no longer wanted by the rest of the world, including all sorts of motorized vehicles. We have thousands of vehicles on the highways that are no longer allowed on European or American highways. Second, there is little enforcement of traffic safety and most drivers are untrained. Functionally unsafe vehicles, together with untrained, uncontrolled drivers, are a no-fail recipe for disaster.

One day I had to travel to a village about five miles from my home to see about some veranda posts for my house. It was September and we were still in the rainy season. I caught a ride in a public transport vehicle, a tin-can-like Renault delivery van that should have long since been recycled into charcoal braziers and window shutters.

In this death trap, flying down the highway at twice a safe speed, we came into a heavy downpour of rain. The windshield wipers didn't work, the windows were all steamed up, and we were rapidly approaching another car that was coming down the highway towards us in our lane.

I thought surely this was the end of the road for me. At the last possible second our driver swerved into the left lane and avoided collision, but with the swerving I could feel our vehicle beginning to go into a tailspin and an inevitable roll into the ditch. Amazingly, that did not happen. Although I didn't see them, angels on both sides were holding up the Renault and keeping the tires in traction with the pavement. Pulling away from that brush with disaster, I was shaken to the core as I visualized what might have happened.

Barley Loaf 5: Mennonite Frugality

Being a frugal person has its own special social challenges because frugality, like beauty, is so open to interpretation by the beholder. Particularly in a culture of materialism and consumerism, frugality and thrift can easily come across as penury, stinginess, and avarice. At a Mennonite congregation where I once was active, I became friends with a brother who shared sentiments about carefully handling one's finances. Another brother, observing us, made the comment: "I thought Andrew Miller [not his real name] was the most tight-fisted guy I ever knew until I met Forrester."

For me, getting four times the mileage out of a dollar naturally belonged to a life of carefully stewarding God's abundance. Had I not been that way, it is unlikely I would have returned to Africa. During my middle years, those working, income-generating years, thrift and frugality enabled me to create assets that eventually were crucial in launching a totally self-supported mission in The Gambia. During those first five years of developing the mission (2000-2004), I operated the mission almost exclusively out of my own financial resources.

Even after I became a fully-supported EMM missionary in 2005, many of the gaps in the mission programs were plugged using my personal resources. Thus, all those years of carefully husbanding my finances were part of the much larger canvas of how the Lord put my life together in a way that enabled me to be a servant in his kingdom. This is quite opposite from viewing my frugality as parsimonious and stingy.

Therefore I make no apologies about driving my Mercedes diesel almost 500,000 miles (the "tractor" as my family called it), wearing shirts that I owned for twenty years, and cutting toothpaste tubes open to clean out the last bit. For me, those choices were neither burdensome nor minimalist; it was just the way God wired me so that I was able to do the work he had ordained for me. To me, frugality has been an enabling experience and a significant factor in the joy of the journey.

A frugal, thrifty, minimalist lifestyle can be driven by two very different motivations—one from above, the other from below. I choose to live a simple and materially minimal life because that is my perception of how Jesus lived incarnationally and in solidarity with the poor. It was how Jesus was best prepared to carry out the work God sent him to do. Jesus both taught and demonstrated the essential inconsistency in giving priority to God's kingdom and at the same time being heavily committed to the acquisition of material comforts and security. You simply can't do both, although many try.

Living frugally and simply is the only consistent way for me to live eschatologically. Christians find themselves living with the paradox of both the already present kingdom of God together with its future consummation. So, is there a "Mennonite frugality"? I think so, provided it derives from an "above" motivation.

Epilogue

The Journey Continues

Overseas long-term missionaries typically serve a term of three to five years, some more, some less. When sensing they have served the purpose for which they were called and commissioned, they return to their native country and re-enter their culture.

After living fourteen years in West Africa, the cement surrounding my feet, gluing me in Africa, became increasingly solid with the passage of time. I choose to retire in Africa for several reasons.

The Push and the Pull

I sense two currents, both heading the same direction: the push to stay away from North America and the pull to remain in Africa.

Culturally, emotionally and in terms of worldview I am, and always will be a North American Mennonite. But there is a push and a pull about that identity that plays significantly into why I chose to remain in Africa.

The Anabaptist-Mennonite identity in North America is moving away from a clear vision to be a radical community of Jesus, an identity confusion that inclines me to stay in Africa. Throughout our five century history Mennonites have struggled to discern what it means to be both in, but not of, the world. God's desire for his people is that they should be a distinct and uncompromised reflection of his righteousness balanced together with God who is missional, welcoming and transforming for all who choose to become part of his people.

In North America there are two notable examples where we are seriously failing to find our way through the maze of reflecting both God's righteousness and design for his new creation and at the same time being facilitators bringing his reign into our here and now: This challenging couplet is our stewardship of God's creation and how to handle his gift of sexuality. Both of these issues are also very important for the church in Africa. It makes me sad to think that it appears that the church in Africa has a significantly better chance of navigating these shoals than the church in North America.

To switch metaphors; the African church, powered by an ancient locomotive, is just chugging out of the darkness of a very long tunnel into the glorious sunshine of God's new day. Coming from the opposite direction we are being met by the North American church heading into the shadows and darkness of the tunnel on a high-speed bullet train. I want to be on the African line.

It is true that the African church has suffered from numerous misdirected fits and starts, but wherever I travel in West Africa, I find a solid core of young adults (mostly under 35) who have seen enough aberrations of church that they know the real thing when they see it. What they are looking for is the radical (back to the roots) church built on the first century life and teachings of Jesus Christ as understood by the first generation eyewitnesses, prophets and apostles, all disciples of Jesus.

With that African milieu, those of us in the Anabaptist tradition are looking at an evangelistic/church growth opportunity in West Africa of the first magnitude. This is a play we must not fumble. And this is why I choose to remain in West Africa.

It's not that everything we do in Africa is somehow right and good. Rather, the African advantage is their openness, teachability and commitment to biblical authority and faithfulness. Africans have great respect for godly elders and leaders in their communities. Africans have a healthy respect and

I am flanked by two students who attended a seminar that I taught in Ghana.

fear of the Lord. All these and more have made it much easier for me to remain in Africa and carry on a teaching ministry in this hunger for righteousness setting of openness and teachability.

Another piece of the decision to stay in West Africa concerned the exit strategy required of all missionaries, particularly pioneer missionaries like myself. EMM policy requires missionaries to eventually leave the field, enabling local church leaders to take over ministries that have been established by the expatriate missionaries. Where the missionaries stay on indefinitely, local leaders may be unwilling or unable to move into leadership. And the church does not move into its next stage of development.

My work in Guinea Bissau reached its eighth year in 2013. By that time we had African leaders in the church who were far more gifted and qualified in church leadership and pastoral ministry in their culture than I. It was time for me to move on.

Normally when the work of a pioneer missionary is completed he moves on to another community to pioneer another mission plant, except that in 2013 I was already well into my eighth decade. I had neither the energy nor the pizzazz to start over again. But neither was I willing to return to the U.S.

Early in 2012 I built a retirement cottage near Ziguinchor, Senegal on the property of missionaries Roger and Rachel Sambou, dear friends since my arrival in Guinea Bissau six years earlier. The setting is in a mostly Christian community about five miles south of Ziguinchor. On the mission grounds there is a church, an orphanage and a conference facility for small groups. The location is good in that it puts me within an easy commute to the Mennonite missions in Gambia and Guinea Bissau. And I have easy travel by ferry to Dakar to make connections to other West Africa locations.

As a withdrawal plan, I made an agreement with EMM to absent myself for a period of one year from the Mennonite mission work I had pioneered in Gambia and Guinea Bissau. Following that I am free to relate to those missions upon their invitation as a Bible teacher and mission consultant. I will not accept any official administrative position in the West Africa church. In May 2013 I took up permanent residence at my home near Ziguinchor and subsequently was commissioned by EMM as a volunteer missionary with an apostolic father role to the West Africa Mennonite work. This was an agreement that made everyone happy, especially the African community who find the departure and abandonment of an elder, father figure, culturally unacceptable.

I look forward to opportunities in assisting the radical church by serving as a Bible teacher locally and in numerous other West African venues.

Beryl's retirement cottage in Bourofaye, Senegal. It is from here that he carries on his ongoing ministry in West Africa.

Appendix

As a senior missionary, I am thrilled to see the younger generation catching the vision to reach Africa. When Andrew Stutzman arrived on the field, I think he was 21 and just a few months out of college. The maturation he demonstrated during the 4-1/2 years he was with us is phenomenal. He is an outstanding model for people of his age group. The days of the cross-cultural missionary are far from over. I pray that God may be calling more of the younger generation just like he called Andrew. Here is his story.

Reflections from a Guinea-Bissau Missionary

I came to Guinea-Bissau with a strong desire to impact God's kingdom and to grow as a Christian through the experience. By God's grace, I believe that both have happened during my 4-1/2 year assignment in Catel.

Serving as a missionary was stretching and challenging in many ways. God used many ministry and leadership experiences to shape me into who I am today. He also taught me many things through the example of the local church. I grew up in a Christian home and have been following Christ for many years. My upbringing and many years of exposure to Christian teaching provided me with a helpful contribution to the young church in Guinea-Bissau. But I was blown away by what I learned from watching them. Many of these new believers still do not have the extensive biblical or theological knowledge that many of us missionaries have, but I was impressed with those who radically practice what they do know.

Guinea-Bissauans taught me about hospitality and relational living. This strength belongs not only to the church but to the culture as a whole. I enjoyed living in a village community where you interact personally with dozens of neighbors every day. In Guinea-Bissau culture, if you walk by someone who is eating, you will be invited to eat with them and expected to accept. I have to admit, this was sometimes frustrating to me. I didn't like to feel obligated to invite uninvited guests to eat my food whenever they happened to drop by during meal times. But I learned to appreciate this aspect of their culture, and I took advantage of their hospitality as many times as I dished it out myself. I traveled a lot during my time in Guinea-Bissau, and I have been hosted overnight by many different families. I always received the same joyful hospitality—including a special meal (they'd often buy a special treat for the occasion), a place to shower, flip flops and a towel if I forgot mine, a clean bed, and good company. I still have much room to improve myself in this area, but I certainly value the model I have seen and experienced over the last few years.

In the context of this relational community, I've come to think of the Catel church as the "city on a hill" that Jesus talks about in his sermon on the mount. In Matthew 5:13-16, Jesus calls his disciples to be the salt of the earth and the light of the world. He tells them that a city on a hill cannot be hidden. Since Catel is such a relational community, and church members are very integrated into the community, the light of the church has always been visibly on display in the village. Changes in believers' lives are immediately noticed in the village by their actions and attitudes.

Evangelism is a strength of the Guinea-Bissau church, and so new believers immediately begin sharing their faith with friends and family in the community. Catel church members are changing the atmosphere in the village. They often take opportunity to speak up against injustice and wrongdoing. They speak truth in the midst of lies. When a group of guys is trying to convince a friend to use witchcraft for some selfish reason, church members will offer a different perspective. I've often seen church members break up fights. I've seen them intercede for children who were being abused. I've seen them take initiative to be peacemakers, mediating conflict between two angry parties. I've seen them council couples who were struggling in their marriages. They take every opportunity to be salt and light in their community. I strive to follow their example in my own community as I move back to the United States.

Gibby Mane, one of the African leaders at the Mennonite Church in Catel, taught me a lot about what it means to be salt and light in a community. The total transformation that God has brought to his life is evident through each interaction he has with people in the village. Small acts of love and grace make a big impact. One day Gibby and I went to visit Catel's Youth Association president concerning some church and mission business. When we arrived at his house, we were greeted by the president's cousin, a woman who had moved to Catel not too long ago. After exchanging simple greetings, the woman teasingly made a sarcastic yet stabbing remark to Gibby. The remark made me feel angry, but Gibby, to whom the remark was aimed, responded gently. With a grin on his face he replied, "Who taught you to talk like this?" The woman responded and the conversation continued as Gibby gently challenged her sarcastic comment.

The woman, knowing Gibby to be a leader of the local church, told him, "You know, I used to go to church." "Really?" Gibby said with an inviting smile. "Yeah," she said, now also smiling. "I knew all the songs. Even now, any church song that you sing I can sing along with you."

As Gibby continued to talk with her, he discovered that she had been an active member of a church for some years but had since become inactive. He also noted that she held the typical "churchianity" understanding of Christianity—that being a Christian is defined by and centered on going to church every Sunday and memorizing certain songs but often lacking a total love and commitment to Christ in all aspects of life. Gibby, maintaining the same inviting smile, pushed her out on this understanding, explaining to her that being a Christian is more than just going to church, but that it is about total surrender to Christ, who transforms every aspect of our lives. By the end of the dialogue the woman was pleasant and smiling, intrigued by Gibby and by the enlightenment of the conversation.

As I watched this conversation unfold I likened it to Jesus' conversation with the Samaritan woman at the well in John 4. Just as Jesus responded to the woman's potentially alienating question about Jews and Samaritans by stretching her understanding of spiritual matters, so Gibby responded to this woman's alienating comment by taking the same opportunity. Gibby reflects Christ as he relates to people in the village. He is a life-giving person, humble and inviting challenging, yet not condemning. He greets people with a smile and often takes opportunity to encourage others and share his love for Christ. He understands that being a disciple is about becoming like Jesus and about allowing him to influence his every decision and his response to each person he encounters. Gibby has become a role model for me in the way he is salt and light in the community.

Another thing that the Catel church has taught me is how to be patient in persecution. Many families are not happy when their son or daughter becomes a Christian. Believers often endure persecution, especially when they first give their lives to Christ. Persecution is usually not physical, but parents will often disrespect, harass, or disown their child for becoming a Christian. Christians risk losing friends as they give up certain sinful activities. New believers know that they must count the cost of becoming a disciple of Christ, because there are deep social consequences. This has made me ask myself why I haven't experienced much persecution myself. Could it be because I haven't lived radically enough for Christ?

The Catel church has also taught and inspired me through their careful evaluation of their own culture. Guinea-Bissau is ethnically diverse and has a beautiful variety of cultures. But as with any culture, there are aspects that honor Christ and others that don't. The Catel church has had to discern which components of their culture they may hold onto and which ones they must let go. For example, the Balanta Mane hold a naming ceremony for a child on the eighth day after birth. Traditionally this includes making sacrifices to the spirits at the front door of the house.

Balanta Mane in the Catel church decided to keep the naming ceremony, but instead of sacrificing to spirits, they invited the church to come over for a couple worship songs, reading of scripture, and a prayer of dedication for the child. Making the change isn't always easy. Convictions of some church members have led them to abstain from certain animistic ceremonies. This has some social consequences, as these ceremonies are important social events in their culture. Conscientious church members battle a lot of peer pressure from people in the community who don't want them to change.

The Catel church has challenged me to evaluate my own culture as I move back to the United States. How do I live as a Christian in the 21st century America? In what ways am I different than those in the community around me? In what ways am I the same? Am I conforming too much? In what ways do I still need to be transformed?

I learned a lot about myself in Guinea-Bissau. I thank God for growing ministry gifts in me as I made myself available to serve him. I discovered that I really have a heart for mentoring and discipling others. I particularly enjoyed helping seekers (those who are not yet committed believers but who are interested in the gospel and are seeking God) and new believers to grow in their understanding of the gospel and in their faith. I discipled youth and young men in a combination of formal and informal settings, and I learned that my ministry was most effective when properly balancing these two approaches. I led Bible studies in group settings as well as one on one. I enjoyed helping people grow in their understanding of scripture and how the Bible influences our lives.

But I discovered that the most effective approach to discipleship is to share life with people. The people who I saw grow the most in their faith during my years in Guinea-Bissau were those who had deep friendships with a missionary or a mature local believer.

A boy named Sadja became my best friend in Guinea-Bissau. We shared life together. He watched how I handled myself in every situation, and I took teaching opportunities to explain to him why I live the way I do. I openly shared with him my joys, successes, pains, struggles, and mistakes. He got an authentic first-hand look at what a follower of Jesus is like—the good, the bad, the ugly, the repentant, and the forgiven. So what he heard in formal Bible teaching he also saw put into practice by me and other Christians around us. I also walked with him as he put his faith into practice—offering a listening ear, encouragement, instruction, challenge, and prayer along the way.

I enjoyed helping people from animistic backgrounds grow in their knowledge of God and to follow Jesus. Guinea-Bissau animists acknowledge the existence of God, but their perception of him is that he is distant, unknowable, and disinterested in our lives. They resort to serving lesser spirits who appeal to their fleshly desires, but who do not have their best interest in mind. As I learned the complexities of their worldview and belief system, I became more effective in sharing the gospel. I began answering the questions they were asking. This was fun! The gospel is good news to animists in every way. It presents a holy, loving, truthful, just, merciful, forgiving, knowable yet surpassing knowledge, all-powerful, all-knowing, omnipresent, creator God as opposed to exploitative, lying, deceitful, accusative, limited, demanding, created spirits. I had a friend who had visited at least half a dozen shamans to seek deliverance from demonic oppression. No one was able to help him. Finally he came to the church. We prayed for him, and he was immediately delivered. I spent the next number of weeks explaining to him from a biblical foundation who God is and who Satan and his demons are. He was fascinated not only with the superior power of God, but also with the contrasting character of God as opposed to Satan. He immediately began sharing the good news with friends and family, and he brought others to the church who were seeking deliverance.

Serving as a missionary in Guinea-Bissau was often difficult. Deeply rooted dependency issues and racial tension carried over into my relationships. I was often frustrated by unreasonable expectations of myself and our organization. I was frequently misunderstood. The culture of America and Guinea-Bissau are on opposite ends of the spectrum. I was accustomed to a lot more privacy in America, and it took some time to adjust to the warmer Guinea-Bissau culture. I grew to appreciate this aspect of the culture. Now that I am back in America I actually miss it.

"It is worth it for the gospel," Beryl once told our missionary team in light of these challenges. These words continue to give me motivation and courage. Indeed, there are many rewards to serving as a missionary. It was a joy and an honor to contribute to something eternal. I love to think about the time when we will all be united in heaven, praising God together for all eternity. I long to be united again on that day with these brothers and sisters who may not have otherwise have had the same opportunity to know Christ. It was a joy to see people understand the gospel in its fullest sense. I think of people like Gibby, who has been holistically transformed into Christ's likeness. He really looks like Christ in the way he relates to people in the community. It was a joy to watch him grow as a leader and to begin taking initiative in leading the church. In many ways I believe that Gibby, in his faith and practice, has even surpassed us missionaries who mentored him. This has been a joy to watch, and I praise God for the transformation he has brought to his life and to others like him. Another reward is the priceless relationships that I built in Guinea-Bissau. There were a few people who really got to know me—people who I shared with mutually, openly, and personally. I treasure these friendships and continue to stay in touch.

My experience as a missionary in Guinea-Bissau has changed the course of my life. These experiences and friendships have shaped me into who I am today. I have been challenged to focus the direction of my life on eternal things. I feel a constant pull to spend the majority of my time chasing after the things of this world. But what a shame it would be to live and die and not make a greater impact. I want to impact God's kingdom. I want to make disciples. And I'm committed to doing that whether I'm in America or across the ocean.

About Beryl Forrester

Beryl Forrester, in his 75th year, is still loving, accepting, embracing and sharing the transformational message of Jesus Christ in West Africa, where he has chosen to live until Jesus calls him to his heavenly home.

He grew up in northern New York State and did his alternate service with MCC in Morocco. He earned a degree in librarianship and worked in public library systems in Vermont and Colorado. Following that he became a fruit farmer in Oregon and from there returned to Africa as a pioneer missionary in Gambia and Guinea Bissau. He continues, under appointment from EMM, as a Bible teacher, contextualizing Anabaptist perspectives among diverse church settings in West Africa.

Contact information

Contact Beryl at berylforrester@gmail.com

For more copies of this book

Additional copies can be ordered online at Amazon.com.

An Amazon page displaying the book can be accessed either by the author's name or the title.

Printed in Germany
by Amazon Distribution
GmbH, Leipzig